On Earth as in Heaven

Other books in the Lutheran Voices series

On Earth as in Heaven

Praying at the Crossroads

Kay Bender Braun

Augsburg Fortress

Minneapolis

To my parents, Mike and Pinky Bender,
who taught me to pray

Purchases of multiple copies of this book are available at a discount from the publisher. For more information, contact the sales department at Augsburg Fortress, Publishers, 1-800-328-4648, or write to: Sales Director, Augsburg Fortress, Publishers, Box 1209, Minneapolis, MN 55440-1209.

Materials for a single or multiple session study of *On Earth as in Heaven* are downloadable free of charge at www.augsburgfortress.org/braun.

Scripture quotations, unless otherwise marked, are from the New Revised Standard Version Bible, copyright © 1989 by the Division of Christian Education of the National Council of Churches of Christ in the USA. All rights reserved. Used by permission. All rights reserved.

Cover image: Wheat Field on Crumhorn Mountain, Maryland, New York. © Rebekah Riley. Used by permission.
Interior artwork reprinted from *Icon Two: Visual Images for Every Sunday* by Lucinda Naylor, © 2004 Augsburg Fortress.

Library of Congress Cataloging-in-Publication Data

Braun, Kay Bender, 1961-
On earth as in heaven : praying at the crossroads / Kay Bender Braun.
    p. cm.
Includes bibliographical references.
ISBN 978-0-8066-8009-5 (alk. paper)
1. Prayer—Christianity. I. Title.

BV210.3.B735 2008
248.3'2—dc22
            2008022179

The paper used in this publication meets the minimum requirements of American National Standard for Information Sciences—Permanence of Paper for Printed Library Materials, ANSI Z329.48-1984.
Manufactured in the U.S.A.

12   11   10   09   08   1   2   3   4   5   6   7   8   9   10

Contents

Preface

When I entered seminary in 1996, it was after several years of avoidance. I knew I did not need to be ordained to serve God, and I was not at all sure how to determine God's will in it all. I journaled, prayed, and talked with others. I went on retreats alone, kept lists of pros and cons, and meditated silently hoping to hear an answer. Ultimately, my mother put it best: "God's yes is louder than your no."

Thank you to my husband, John, who did not marry me thinking I'd ever become a pastor, and to my children, Michael and Thomas, who join me in prayer, give me reasons to pray, and have supported this project. Thank you to the people of St. Petri-Hope Lutheran Church, who, by praying this prayer each Sunday and at various crossroads in their lives, fueled the writing.

The Lutheran expression of my faith, a return to my roots, was cemented at the Lutheran Theological Seminary at Philadelphia, through various professors and classmates. I owe a debt of gratitude to the Rev. Dr. Timothy Wengert, who listened to the first babblings of an outline and encouraged me to write the manuscript. What you hold in your hands would not have been possible without Susan Johnson and Cynthia Nelson. Thank you both for patiently editing the manuscript into printable form. This book represents a continuing desire to be in relationship with God and put God first as I face decisions at every point in life. There is no simple answer to "what is God's will"? It will be different for each reader. Consider this volume my attempt at making sense of, "so many choices, which way to turn?"

1

Praying at the Crossroads

In my family, where there is a pool, there is often an energetic, competitive game of "Monkey in the Middle." Some may be more familiar with dry-land versions of the game, like "Pickle" or "Keep Away," but "Monkey in the Middle" played in water, allows for more flexible movements. Two folks play keep-away from a third, who stands in between. If the one in the middle catches the ball, he or she exchanges places with the one who threw it. It's an apt image for discernment and decision making in my life: one player is God and the other player is practicality, reason, or emotions, and I am *always* in the middle. My emotions are the fuel that keeps me playing, and my gut and my instincts tell me when to move, when to reach beyond me, and when to wait. Timing and spacing are everything. If I am too close to opportunity, God is not reachable. If I stand too far from the opportunity, it flies over my head. It's a tricky game.

Discerning God's Will
Discernment is one of those theological words that flies over the heads of some but is reached for and longed for by others. Webster defines it as: "to perceive something hidden or obscure; to comprehend mentally."[1] It is a word that takes on other layers of meaning depending on several individual factors. First, what is your perspective on life itself? Are you an observer or an active participant? That is, do things seem to just "happen to you," or do you sense that your choices and outlook influence outcomes? Second, what is your relationship with God? Is God the boss, the one in control of your life? Or, is God your advisor or friend? Or perhaps, is God the co-creator of your life? Third, what is your background, your personal religious experience? If it seems that

you often observe what happens to you and feel powerless to influence it, if it seems that God is the boss and you have no say, then discernment may be a foreign concept. Why should you spend the time figuring out what's next or what's right? Whatever is going to happen will happen. But if your background values quiet introspection, then perhaps, if given enough time, you will intuit an answer. If you believe that God is the giver of all things—your intellect included—and you see yourself as a participant in creation, then discernment is something for which you pray and long, as it means your life and God's will are in the same zip code, if not on the same path.

So is discernment forever a mystery? Or is it a new realization about an old situation? An "aha" moment? Might it also be the mental comprehension of a good choice, relating to decision-making? Some would have us believe, given the hidden nature of the act, that discernment is entirely divine revelation. Others may relate to the obscure nature of discernment and suggest that deep contemplation or meditation will help us perceive. Still others would suggest a mental checklist, a tangible weighing of the pros and cons of the decision, as well as the pros and cons of the consequences to you and others.

In my personal and in my professional life, I have observed a variety of approaches to discernment. For example, a young man I know was trying to decide whether to attend a popular, prestigious college, or pursue his one true love: baseball. The young man talked to his parents, his coach, his counselor, and his friends. Receiving a rejection letter from a large school helped him decide to pursue sports at a smaller college. Finally, it came down to two choices: a school far away with a better reputation or one closer to home. After visiting the school close by, the young man was excited about the coach's creativity and personal approach, and he could envision himself as a student there. At the second school, the coach did not respond to inquiries. The young man made his decision based on circumstances (rejection and acceptance), information (opinions from those with whom he talked) and emotions (the contentment that came with imagining himself at the school).

A couple came to me for pre-wedding discussions. For the man, it was a second marriage. For the woman, it was her first. A church setting with family was important. When describing family and relationships, the husband-to-be admitted frustration that one of his children had come back home to live and was not motivated to seek work or be independent. At my urging, the couple made a balance sheet of sorts: pros and cons to marrying now versus marrying later. Through the exercise, they realized they needed to choose between their own relationship and their relationship with children. They chose each other and delayed the wedding until they could establish a home with just the two of them.

Personally, I have tried a variety of decision strategies when faced with choices in life. I have meditated in silence, freeing my mind of conscious thought and hoping an answer will emerge from the quiet. Sometimes I have come out refreshed with a new idea; other times the meditation has ended with a shopping list breaking into the reverie. I have tried silent, word-by-word contemplation of scripture (both assigned texts and the random "open the Bible and point to a verse" methods). Sometimes a new thought or perspective on the passage has emerged, but other times I have just gotten bored, wanting to read more or following a cross reference to a whole other passage. I have logically listed pros and cons of decisions, then put the list away for a while to return and see which side carries more weight. But how do you weigh potential for personal growth and fulfillment against spousal employment or schools for the kids? How do you allow for the gut feelings involved? I have often polled others for an opinion. Sometimes I get a new perspective, other times the responses are fifty/fifty and I am left confused.

Then there's the random approach. When preparing for the first-call assignment process in the ELCA, my husband and I were stumped as to what regions I'd be willing to serve. I had come from the North Carolina Synod to attend seminary in Philadelphia and always thought we would return south. My husband was the primary wage earner and our oldest child was attending school at an academic magnet. The ELCA preferred that I be open to serving anywhere. My heart and family preferred that we return south. One evening, after having tried each of the discernment tools already mentioned, John and I got out a map of the United States, closed our eyes, and pointed randomly. Our fingers landed in Maryland! Having tried and appreciated all those approaches, I finally experienced an "aha" of my own. What if I put and kept God at the center of a pending decision? And what if, with my Christian roots, I looked at the life and example of Jesus to guide how to discern God's will and thus make my decision? What might that look like?

Biblical Models of Discernment

The first time I visited a colleague in Nebraska I was struck by the vastness of the landscape. To walk the "block" was a three-mile hike around the boundaries of a farm. When I stood at the "corner," as far as I could see in any direction, the landscape looked identical. That's often what it seems like when a major decision looms. As we stand at the crossroads, things look the same in every direction. There is no billboard telling us what to do, no arrow pointing in the right direction. But we are not alone. If we look to scripture, we find biblical giants, pillars of the faith who stood at difficult crossroads too. In Genesis, chapter 6, there was not a cloud in the sky when God first told Noah that God would destroy the earth (verse 13). Then God told Noah to build an ark, and God gave him the list of what building materials to use and how big to make the ark. When God announced that a flood would destroy anything that had breath, Noah had a crucial decision before him: enjoy the beautiful weather or build the ark? When God told Noah the rains would come in seven days and it was time to enter the ark, Noah faced a critical decision: pay attention to the absence of raindrops or obey God? In verse 22 we find his decision: "Noah did all this; he did all that God commanded him." As a result, Noah and his family were spared.

In Exodus 3, when God told Moses on Mount Horeb to go to Pharaoh and demand the people's release from slavery in Egypt, Moses stood at a crossroads. As he processed the instruction, he first declined the opportunity. After all, he was gainfully employed as a shepherd. Moses wanted to first gather as much information as he could and then, as he heard more, he resisted the idea. He had lots of questions and a few protests too: Who do I say is sending me? (Exod. 3:13). What if they do not believe me? (Exod. 4:1). But I'm not the best speaker you could choose! (Exod. 4:10). Please send someone else! (Exod.

4:13). Finally in verse 18 we discover that Moses relented, went to his father-in-law, gave notice, and headed to Egypt.

Jesus' Model

Throughout the Gospels, Jesus' time and ministry included teaching and healing that required him to be in constant touch with individuals and crowds of people, and time alone, apart from the crowds and even his disciples. We can see this movement, between crowd and quiet, in the Gospel of Mark. In chapter three, after healing a man in a crowded synagogue, Jesus left with his disciples, but a throng followed. "He told his disciples to have a boat ready for him because of the crowd, so that they would not crush him; for he had cured many, so that all who had diseases pressed upon him to touch him" (Mark 3:10). Again, in the next chapter, while Jesus taught beside the sea, a large crowd gathered, so he got in a boat and pushed away from shore to teach (Mark 4:1). In chapter 9, we read how Jesus took Peter, James, and John up a mountain apart from the others (Mark 9:2). It would seem then, that our own discernment, indeed our lives of faith, could follow the same healthy approach that Jesus modeled: allowing for time with community, in corporate worship and service, followed by time alone for personal devotions and prayer.

If Jesus had spent three years going from crowd to crowd, from healing request to healing request, he likely would have burned out. Conventional wisdom tells caregivers to care for themselves first. Rest, nourishment, and reflection are ways to provide that care. Likewise today, if you work in a loud, busy environment, a chance for quiet is a blessing. Those who work double shifts are routinely given several days off along the way to recuperate and recharge. Going from task to task, from event to event, from person to person with no break does not give you a chance to enjoy the blessings of the day or reflect on what might make tomorrow better.

Finally, when faced with the most challenging, gut-wrenching moment in his three-year ministry, Jesus turned to prayer. In agony, he prayed, "Father, if you are willing, remove this cup from me; yet, not my will but yours be done" (Luke 22:42). Not every choice we make is a life or death decision, as it was for Jesus in the Garden of Gethsemane. The salvation of others may not hang in the balance as we decide what to do, and yet our decision might very well influence how someone perceives God or how someone interprets God's action in the world. When faced with a major decision we can look to Jesus' model of relationship with his Father, of time alone and prayer.

Prayer and Discernment

We too stand at a crossroads. Whether facing employment or retirement choices, vocational or family choices, health or treatment choices, the landscape may look the same in every direction, with no clear marker as to what to choose. These complicated choices call for faithful discernment and a responsible decision without knowing the full consequences, without knowing how our choice will shape the future for us or for those we love. As Christians, we hear that we are to surround such times with prayer. Often, that instruction leaves us saying, with the disciples, "Lord, teach us to pray, as John taught his disciples" (Luke 11:1). What follows is what we call the Lord's Prayer (Matt. 6:9-13 and Luke 11:1-4).

In Matthew 6, Jesus' instructions on prayer came as part of the Sermon on the Mount, in which Jesus shared directives on many key matters. Jesus acknowledged, as he answered the disciples' request, that their Father knew what they needed before they asked. So why bother to pray? If, as Jesus teaches, God knows what we need before we pray, then is prayer just a fruitless exercise, little more than talking to ourselves? Imagine a seven-year-old child, just waking up in the morning, after sleeping ten hours. He staggers down the stairs, rubs his eyes and sees Dad in the kitchen. "I'm hungry," he says. "Can I have pancakes for breakfast?" Certainly Dad knows the child is hungry, and certainly Dad knows pancakes are the child's favorite. So why does the child bother to ask? The child asks because the child believes Dad will respond. The child asks because the child has experience that indicates Dad is a caring provider. When the child asks, the child shows trust in the father. The child asks, not because Dad would never guess in a million years what the child needs first thing in the morning, but because Dad's track record shows him he can ask. The child doesn't need to use a lot of words or an impressive vocabulary. The child only has to ask. The same is true for us. Our petitions to God do not have to be flowery or offered to impress. They don't need to be wordy. Jesus said, "Pray then like this." And what we know as the Lord's Prayer followed.

In the Large Catechism, Martin Luther put it this way: "Let this be said . . . in order that we may learn above all to value prayer as a great and precious thing and may properly distinguish between vain babbling and asking for something. By no means do we reject prayer, but we do denounce the utterly useless howling and growling, as Christ himself rejects and forbids great wordiness."[2]

At whatever crossroads you find yourself, using whatever discernment tools are most helpful to you, I hope you will place the Lord's Prayer in your toolbox. Maybe your choice is between two options, or maybe the choices seem limitless. This book will not give you answers particular to your circumstances. But I hope that this book will give you new eyes and insight to connect an old prayer to your new situation. May the Lord's Prayer guide the decisions you make and the steps you take.

Connecting with God's Word

Read again the Lord's Prayer from Matt. 6:9-13 and Luke 11:1-4. Note similarities and differences. With what petition do you most resonate? What petition most baffles or challenges you?

Considering the Crossroads

1. What is prayer? Is there any situation or topic that would not be appropriate for prayer?
2. When and why do you most often pray?
3. Is it okay to pray for yourself? Why or why not?
4. In the Matthew version of the Lord's Prayer, we pray that God would rescue us from the "evil one." Do you appreciate this wording or are you challenged by it? Why?
5. Have you ever prayed the Lord's Prayer when trying to make a decision? If so, did it help you? Why or why not?

Our Father in heaven. . . .

2

The Perfect Parent

Three words interrupted my sandbox play, dramatically changed the course of my day, and caused me to freeze in my tracks: "Katherine Swift Bender!" When I heard my full, given name, I knew I was in trouble, and those nearby knew it too. Perhaps it was something I had not done; many times it was something I *had* done, and it was time to face the consequences. By the same token, when I heard my mother softly intone a favorite nickname, "Katy-bug," I felt that, at least in that moment, our relationship was comfortable and relaxed and that I was likely to get a hug. No one had to explain all this to me. It was something I knew from being in close and constant relationship with my mother.

When we anticipate a major transition or decision, it is common to think we face it alone. Praying the Lord's Prayer in those times reminds us from the very first phrase that we are not alone, but joined with others in community. This prayer came out of close, constant relationships: between disciples and their Lord, between our Lord and his Father, and between those who pray it and their God. It is intended for those in relationship with God. It is not so much a prayer for non-believers or seekers as for believers who already know God and call God "Father." We discover in this prayer words between a Son and a Father who are close, not estranged and certainly not strangers. It is a prayer from God-with-us, Emmanuel, to God the Father almighty, creator of heaven and earth. We find in this prayer, not a passing suggestion between those whose paths cross for a brief time, but a powerful response from a teacher to a student's request. The request came not from a student who sat in class once a week for ten weeks, but a student who relinquished his familiar family and vocational life to follow, travel, and live with the teacher for three years. This prayer begins with a snapshot, if you will, from the godly family photo album, for this phrase reveals that Jesus was so close to his father, that he called him *Abba* (Aramaic for "Daddy"). It was a name associated with intimacy, closeness, and familiarity, as opposed to a more formal name, Yahweh. To call God "Father" is akin to calling someone "dear," or calling a young girl "Katy-bug."

Our Father: Praying in Community

The Lord's Prayer begins with three key words. Three simple, but sometimes problematic words: *our*, *Father*, and *heaven*. The first word—*our*—can be a stumbling block for many North American, twenty-first century believers. It seems we are not as focused on community as much as on the individual. Instant gratification is the order of the day. We want things now; we want them quickly and easily. In today's world, worship often takes a backseat to kids' sports or sleeping in or working overtime. Time is precious, so we jettison corporate worship. Watching a TV evangelist is quicker and more convenient than going to church. Since we can sit at home and read scripture and even sing hymns, why must we go to a church for worship? Somewhere along the way, we have come to think that it is enough for us to believe as individuals in isolation. We think, in the interest of time, we can skip coming together as a community worshiping and praying together. We approach God, saying, "Listen to *me*; answer *my* prayer" and forget that the prayer we are given begins with the very concept we ignore: we are to come to this prayer as a community; we pray together *our*.

This tendency toward privatization and individual piety, the tendency to skip the community worship experience in favor of private devotions, also can influence the very way we approach discernment and decision making. "It is *my* decision, and I do not need you," we might think. "This is a practical, logical decision; I do not need God's help." Or, we may feel that turning our decision making over to God implies that we are weak (which we are), and we don't really want to acknowledge weakness. We don't want to turn over our decision making to anyone else, including God. It's not what one does in our society.

Even as we pray, then, we focus on ourselves. Do we not, as a deadline approaches, find ourselves crying out, "What am *I* to do?" "How do *I* know what is right?" "Show *me* the way!" Discernment then becomes hard work, a puzzle to solve, a problem to overcome, and it is up to the individual to muster enough energy and brains and resolve to come to the right answer. Discernment becomes something we do alone. At one time or another, many of us find ourselves thinking, "If only I pray hard enough, pray long enough, find the right balance between the positives and negatives, then I will know what to do, then I will know which way to go." If discernment does not become work, it becomes almost mystical, a goal that only the holiest can reach. The word *mysticism* comes from a Greek word meaning, "to conceal." The dictionary defines *mysticism* as "the belief that direct knowledge of God, spiritual truth, or ultimate reality can be attained through subjective experience (as intuition or insight)."[1] The Lord's Prayer instead points us to each other and to God. Granted, some decisions must eventually be made by just one person, such as, whether to quit a job or to enter a partnership. But even in those cases, prayers and counsel from the community are important. Many more decisions are best made within a community that prays together, studies scripture together, and shares the sacraments and supports one another within a life of worship and faithful living. "What am *I* to do?" is not as healthy as praying together, as a community, "*Our* Father."

The Lord's Prayer was first given to a group of people, not an individual. It begins where discernment begins: with the recognition that the individual is part of a bigger "our." God's intention that we not live in isolation is evident from Genesis, when "God created humankind in his image, in the image of God he created them; male and female he created them. God blessed them, and God said to them, 'Be fruitful and multiply'" (Gen.1:27-28). Or again, when God declared that man should not be alone and created woman (Gen. 2:18). As part of a believing community, we are not alone in our prayer or decision making. In Matthew 18:15-18, Jesus gave the disciples a model for resolving disputes among believers. After the instruction, he reassured them, "For where two or three are gathered in my name, I am there among them"(Matt. 18:20). Jesus called twelve, rather than ministering in isolation. Jesus gave this prayer to the twelve. We pray together, "*Our* Father."

Our *Father*: Praying in Relationship

The Lord's Prayer begins with the recognition that we are bound together, united in community. It continues with the realization that the one praying is in relationship with God. We don't pray to just anybody. When we pray, we aren't conversing with a person or talking to a loved one who has died or musing to ourselves. We pray, as a community, to our *Father*, the one who creates, provides, and cares.

In first-century Palestine, when Jesus taught the disciples this prayer, it was commonly understood that the father in the household was the property owner, the one with status in the community and authority in the family. Indeed, one of our biblical images of God as father comes from Jesus' parable of the lost son (Luke 15:11-32), where the father gives his young son an early inheritance, watches him leave home and squander it, then return in shame. Our vision of God as father is like that of the father who runs down the road, robes flying and arms wide open, to welcome the son back. In our society, where too many fathers are unknown, missing, neglectful, or abusive, still we are bold to pray, "Our *Father*," reclaiming a relationship that reflects care, welcome, and forgiveness.

When we pray "Our *Father*," we pray knowing we are not God, but looking and praying to God who created us, understands us, and has the answers to questions we raise. We are God's children, who turn to our loving parent for answers beyond our comprehension. We profess our belief in God the caring creator and protector as Luther described in his explanation to the first article of the Apostles' Creed: "I believe that God has created me together with all that exists. God has given me and still preserves my body and soul: eyes, ears and all limbs and senses; reason and all mental faculties. God protects me against all danger and shields and preserves me from all evil. And all this is done out of pure, fatherly, and divine goodness and mercy."[2]

Praying to the Divine: Our Father *in Heaven*

Lest we confuse or belittle this one to whom we pray, we pray, "Our Father *in heaven*." Ours is not an ordinary father. This is not a father with the option to divorce, abandon, or neglect his children. This is our heavenly Father who created us and all things, who created relationships, who went to extraordinary means to insure that what we as a human community destroy and neglect is restored and reconciled over and over again. "Our Father *in heaven*" turns our eyes from ourselves and toward a powerful, creative God. The words turn our gaze from the tunnel vision of our present surroundings and circumstances toward eternity. We begin this prayer, as we begin our discernment, looking together—not in isolation—to one greater than us who is not focused on petty human desire. By praying, "Our Father in heaven," we turn our discernment over to God who has no beginning and no end, whose kingdom is found in heaven and on earth.

The Lord's Prayer begins with three simple words: *our, father,* and *heaven*. Each word can create a mental or emotional barrier today, based on individual experiences with congregations or earthly parents, but each word can also deepen the invitation to pray. Perhaps we hear *our* as a barrier, thinking that the decision we face is private, a decision that affects and influences only *me*. Yet *our* connects the individual with every other believer who prays, reminding us that we are not alone, joining us to one another. Perhaps we hear *father* as a barrier, because the best of human fathers fail us. Yet *father* also connects us with a caring Creator who provides all that we need and who loves us as an attentive parent loves a child. Perhaps we hear *heaven* as a barrier, because we fancy ourselves too intelligent, too rational, and too scientifically minded to embrace what some view as a wishful and wistful concept. Instead, let us reclaim *heaven* as a promise that we as baptized believers will dwell forever in God's love. Let us accept the gift of God's presence, not fretting over location or dimension, but boldly praying, "Our Father in heaven."

"Our Father in heaven" centers us on the God who creates us to be in relationship, to live and worship and discern and decide in a community setting. "Our Father in heaven" focuses us on one who is in authority but still an attentive, loving caregiver. "Our Father in heaven" turns our eyes from ourselves and toward God even when, and especially when, we stand at the crossroads of a major decision.

Connecting with God's Word

Read Psalm 8. This psalm offers us a glimpse of our place in creation. It upholds our worth as human beings while clearly reminding us that God is God, and we, though crowned with honor, are not God. When does God seem the most real to you? When do you feel the closest to God?

Consider the Crossroads

1. How might you respond to someone who says, "I do not need to worship or be part of a congregation to be a faithful person?"
2. How might being part of the "our" help you as you make a crucial decision in your life or the life of your family?
3. What was your earliest concept of heaven? Does this give you the perspective that God is near and involved or distant as you face the decision that lies ahead?

Hallowed be your name. . . .

3

It's All in a Name

When I was pregnant, my husband and I were very intentional about what we would name our child. We checked all the books and considered our family trees. We discussed the variety of names and the significance of their meanings. Different names meant different things, and we took them all into account. If the baby was a boy, we could name him after his grandfather, Michael, which means "beloved." If it was a girl, she could be given her mother's name, Katherine, which means "pure." It wasn't an easy decision. There's a lot to a name.

Scripture puts a great deal of emphasis on the significance of names too. Isaac was named for his parent's laughter at having a child in their old age, and Moses' name came from his being drawn out of the waters of the Nile by Pharaoh's daughter. Sometimes names were even changed at God's request, as in the case of Abram and Sarai (Abraham and Sarah). Other times God instructed parents as to what name they should give their children, Jesus being the prime example. Often a name reflected a personality trait. For instance, Thomas, whose name means "twin," expressed two sides of himself when first he wanted proof that Jesus, who had died, was really alive and standing before him, but then declared, "my Lord and my God." Peter, whose name means "rock," crumbled under pressure and denied knowing Jesus, but his faith and declaration of Jesus as Messiah became the cornerstone of Christian faith. And what of names for the Son of God? *Emmanuel* means "God with us." *Messiah* means "anointed." Savior has the biblical connotation of a political ruler who has come to rescue those who are oppressed.

God's Name Is Holy

The second petition of the Lord's Prayer also talks about names, one special name, the name of God. When we pray, "hallowed be your name," we pray that God's name would be holy. When we pray, "hallowed be your name," we pray that God's name would be consecrated, set apart, and revered. In religious history, the name for God that best captures this concept is from Hebrew tradition—Yahweh. Yahweh is a holy name, so holy that it could not be spoken and was written YHWH, with no vowels, unpronounceable. In the presence of one so holy, one acts differently, as seen several places in scripture. Abraham fell on his face in God's presence (Genesis 17). Moses removed his shoes when standing before the burning bush (Exodus 3). In the vision that is part of the prophet Isaiah's call to ministry, seraphs in God's presence covered their faces and their feet (Isaiah 6). Even so, holy does not mean inaccessible. God intervened before Abraham could sacrifice his only son, Isaac. As the Israelites traversed the wilderness, Moses knew God was nearby; God was tangibly present through a pillar of fire by night and a cloud by day. The Holy One touched Isaiah's lips with coal and made the prophet holy. God is holy, yes, but God is still in relationship with mere humans.

"Hallowed be your name" is part of a prayer that was prayed within the context of relationship, shared within the context of relationship, and prayed today within the understanding of relationship. Jesus the Son of God prayed to the Father. Jesus the teacher gave the prayer to his students. Those of us praying it today are those who believe, who have a relationship with the Triune God and pray it as part of our communal relationship with other believers. Even when prayed in the quiet, secluded confines of our room at home, the prayer connects us with Christians of every time and place. So when, for us, is God's name hallowed or holy? In Luther's understanding, as expressed in the Large Catechism, "God's name is already holy without our prayer. Indeed, it is hallowed in the teaching, hearing, and living of God's Word."[1] If that is the case, then God's name is hallowed when believers gather for worship, when believers hear the word of grace through the sacraments, words of absolution, and prayers of the faithful. Likewise, discernment and decision making, while ultimately falling on the shoulders of the one who must say yes or no or state a choice, does not often occur within a vacuum, but within the relationships and connections between ourselves and others.

Barriers to Understanding God's Holiness

For some, the concept of God's holiness might seem like a barrier keeping them from God. It would not be enough, in the face of the burning bush, to take off their shoes; they would never believe they could even approach the bush. Likewise God's holiness might keep you from praying. In the Large Catechism, Martin Luther addressed these feelings of inadequacy, when he wrote, "We allow ourselves to be impeded and deterred by such thoughts as these: 'I am not holy enough or worthy enough; if I were as righteous and holy as St. Peter or St. Paul, then I would pray.' Away with such thoughts!"[2] Feelings of doubt or unworthiness need not keep us from praying. In his letter to the Romans, Paul indicated that when we are stumped, the Holy Spirit takes over. "Likewise the Spirit helps us in our weakness; for we do not know how to pray as we ought, but that very Spirit intercedes with sighs too deep for words" (Rom. 8:26).

If we can pray that God's name be holy, then it makes sense that by our words and actions we could also dishonor God's name. In fact, Luther discussed this at some length in the Large Catechism:

> In the first place, then, it is profaned when people preach, teach and speak in the name of God anything that is false and deceptive, using his name to dress up their lies and make them acceptable; this is the worst desecration and dishonor of his name. Likewise, when people grossly misuse the divine name as a cover for their shame, by swearing, cursing, conjuring, etc. In the next place, it is also profaned by an openly evil life and wicked works, when those who are called Christians and God's people are adulterers, drunkards, gluttons, jealous persons, and slanderers.[3]

It seems, then, that while one might pray, "Our Father in heaven" from the head, by rote or repetition, that to pray "hallowed be your name" expects that the heart and the actions of the one praying will fit the prayer. If it really means I can only pray that God's name be holy if and only if I lead a holy life, then I give up, it is impossible. Except that as a Lutheran, I know and believe that holiness, like faith, is a gift from God made real to me through the Holy Spirit. From Luther's explanation of the Third Article of the Creed in the Small Catechism, I am reassured: "I believe that by my own understanding or strength I cannot believe in Jesus Christ my Lord or come to him, but instead the Holy Spirit has called me through the gospel, enlightened me with his gifts, made me holy and kept me in the true faith, just as he calls, gathers, enlightens, and makes holy the whole Christian church on earth."[4]

Another way to look at it, for Luther, is that praying, "hallowed be your name," means keeping the second commandment ("You shall not take the name of the Lord your God in vain"). In addition to all the ways enumerated above, it is also possible, wrote Luther in the Large Catechism, to abuse or misuse God's name in "business affairs and in matters involving money, property, and honor, whether publicly in court or in the marketplace or wherever someone commits perjury and swears a false oath in God's name or by his own soul."[5] I would take this a step further. I believe it is possible to use God's name lightly even when we think we are honoring it. That is, by consulting God on small matters that we might as easily decide on our own, it does not necessarily hallow God's name. Kathy and Joe told us they would get back to us in a few days regarding our dinner invitation. "We need to pray about it," they said. Myrtle says she routinely prays before leaving the mall parking lot as to which route to take home. When Luther acknowledged in the First Article of the Creed that God created us, he got very specific: "God has given me and still preserves my body and soul: eyes, ears, and all limbs and senses; reason and all mental faculties."[6] There will be routine matters for which we can use our powers of logic and reasoning and make a decision for ourselves. What to cook for dinner depends on what is in the house or the funds available to go shopping. Which way to return home can be decided by listening to a radio traffic report. You get the picture.

Honoring God in Our Decisions

As you stand at the crossroads of a decision, is there an option that honors God and God's name? Is there an option that relies on deception, short cuts, or white lies? Which is easier to choose? Consider Frank's situation: he and his family have been struggling this year. His wife was laid off just before his youngest child started college. Frank took several part-time jobs to make up the difference in income. As tax time approached, he debated whether or not to report the income from his cash-payment jobs. Or Daniel: he had just started a new job and felt like perhaps he was in over his head. Maybe he should not have said he had a business degree when he had just begun night classes. Should he own up? What would happen if he did?

Many decisions are not that clear-cut, but whatever we choose should offer glory and praise to God's name. Our decisions should not require us to hide our faith or compromise our beliefs. Gloria had noticed large sums of cash missing from her room during the last month, but she was afraid to confront her niece, Angie. One evening, when Angie came home stoned, Gloria had a tough decision to make. Call the police about the thefts? Ignore the facts and hope Angie grew out of it? Kick Angie out of the house with no further action?

As a woman of faith, Gloria wanted to do the right thing. She wanted to honor God's name in her decision. She considered that one of the Ten Commandments is "You shall not steal" (Exod. 20:15). She also read Paul's first letter to the Corinthians, where he wrote, "Do you not know that your body is a temple of the Holy Spirit within you, which you have from God, and that you are not your own? For you were bought with a price; therefore glorify God in your body" (1 Cor. 6:19-20). Gloria turned Angie in, and the judge allowed treatment in lieu of jail time. Today, Angie continues to struggle, but she is on the right path.

This chapter began with a discussion of names and their various meanings and associations. This petition we pray in the Lord's Prayer, "hallowed be your name," requires us to remember there is only one name that is holy. God's name is holy, not mine or yours, not the boss's or the neighbor's. God's name is holy, not the name of the one expecting your decision pronto. And God's name is hallowed in those times when you draw near to the throne of grace with others, when you gather as part of the communion of saints.

Connecting with God's Word

Read Luke 4:14-21. In this passage, the first place that Jesus visited after having put the devil in his place back in the wilderness was the synagogue in Nazareth. Filled with the Spirit, he went to the house of worship on the Sabbath, "as was his custom." Here Jesus read from the prophet Isaiah, and after rolling up the scroll and taking his seat, he proclaimed to those gathered, "Today this scripture has been fulfilled in your hearing." Luther said that God's name becomes holy in and among us, "whenever the Word of God is taught clearly and purely and we, as God's children, also live holy lives according to it."[7] While it is certainly possible to learn from God's Word through television, radio, and the Internet, there is also value in gathering with others to hear God's Word preached and taught at church.

In this time of technology, when everyone has a phone, carries their music collection with them, and prefers Power Point presentations to handouts, what are the benefits and advantages to reading scripture aloud or hearing it read? What does your faith life gain by gathering with other believers?

Considering the Crossroads

1. With what name or description for God (for example: Creator, God, Elohim, Father, Lord, Protector, Almighty) do you most resonate or connect? Why? How does your answer affect the way you pray?
2. As you stand at the crossroads of a decision, how does the possibility of God's name being hallowed within a community, within a worship experience, resonate with you or rub you the wrong way? Why?

Your kingdom come. . . .

4

It's Not about Me

The newsroom of the daily paper was a microcosm of business practices. Day-to-day operations included the corporate hierarchy, revenue-based decisions, and the success of a few built on the hard work of many others. Within that system, reporters and photographers knew the chain of command, the appropriate ladder of communication, and everyone's clearly defined duties. Except that when the editor-in-chief entered the newsroom, it upset the order and structure. He drew energy from the people around him and then seemingly toppled the order as easily as swirling winds topple lawn furniture. The newsroom was his kingdom. The reporters, editors, and designers were his subjects. They knew not to cross him. They knew their best ideas would become his, because at his best, he did not think outside the office, much less the box. And while he was not the CEO, he operated as if the workplace were his domain. This boss, who loved the job so much, loved it almost to death. He struggled with stress; his blood pressure was high. He was hospitalized and eventually had to retire from the kingdom he tried so hard to create.

Images of God's Kingdom

Just whose kingdom is it? The psalmist writes, "The earth is the Lord's and all that is in it, the world, and those who live in it" (Ps. 24:1). It is clear: the kingdom is God's. The earth and everything we see and everyone we meet belong to God. But too often we decide that our life or our job or our church is *our* kingdom. We act as if we are in charge; we think we are in control. *We* decide purpose and priorities; *we* determine the future. That might make for efficient management, but it is not in keeping with the teachings and example of Jesus.

Time and again Jesus discussed the kingdom of God, a kingdom where God is in charge, and a kingdom that draws near as he, Jesus, comes near. In Luke 12, Jesus encouraged the disciples to quit worrying about food or clothes or possessions. "Instead, strive for his kingdom, and all these things will be given to you as well" (Luke 12:31). In Matthew, Jesus discussed the kingdom through several short parables. He compared the kingdom of heaven to a treasure in a field (Matt. 13:44), to a merchant in search of pearls (Matt. 13:45), and to a net that catches fish of every kind (Matt. 13:47). In Matthew 18, when the disciples asked, "Who is the greatest in the kingdom of heaven?" Jesus replied, "Truly I tell you, unless you change and become like children, you will never enter the kingdom of heaven" (Matt. 18:3). In Luke, when Jesus sent seventy ahead of him in pairs, the message to those they met—both those who welcomed them and those who did not—was the same: "the kingdom of God has come near" (Luke 10:11). The kingdom, then, is a reality that comes near as Jesus comes near; it is present now but not yet complete. It is a valuable thing, inclusive of all, and best approached with the trust and the innocence of a child.

The cosmos is God's creation. In the Lord's Prayer, the kingdom for which we pray, the kingdom already among us, is God's. This petition is not a longing for some far-off, remote location. God's kingdom came during creation. God's kingdom became earthy when God came to be among us in Jesus. God's kingdom is as close as the Spirit moving in and through us. We pray *your* kingdom come, not *my* kingdom come.

Trouble with the Terminology

A kingdom implies a ruler. A kingdom implies an order. A kingdom implies a system in which those not in charge turn to and defer to the one who is in charge, the king. We do not pray, your committee come. We do not pray, your suggestion or proposal come. We do not pray, your democracy or republic come. We pray, knowing one is in charge, and that one is not us. The word *kingdom* may sound archaic to our twenty-first century ears. Perhaps we picture a velvet throne and golden crown adorned with precious jewels. Perhaps we hear the lion from *The*

Wizard of Oz singing his longing to be king of the forest. Many monarchies today appear to be merely ceremonial, with elected officials doing all the ruling business. Kings (and queens) often are figureheads and not much more. We don't really hold kings in high regard. In fact, the closest we come to familiarity with royalty nowadays is perhaps through the tabloid escapades of the royal family in England. Kings and kingdoms just don't seem to be in our vocabulary anymore.

Those in Jesus' time seemed to have had a little trouble with the terminology too. When Jesus rode into Jerusalem on what we call Palm Sunday, the people were expecting a king. Indeed, they even cried out, "Hosanna! Blessed is the one who comes in the name of the Lord—the King of Israel!" (John 12:13). But Jesus didn't ride in on a horse and chariot like any self-respecting, conquering ruler would. Instead, he came plodding along on a donkey's colt. His humble entry was the antithesis of everything the ancient world deemed kingly. In Luke 23, when Jesus was brought before Pilate, he was accused of perverting the nation, saying that he was the Messiah, a king. "Then Pilate asked him, 'Are you the king of the Jews?' He answered, 'You say so'" (v. 3). Later, while Jesus was on the cross, soldiers mocked him, saying, "If you are the King of the Jews, save yourself!" (v. 37). Indeed, Jesus was crucified under an inscription that read, "This is the King of the Jews" (v. 38). But what picture, then, do we have of that king? Instead of purple robes, Jesus was stripped of his tunic. Instead of the bling of a crown, he wore a crown of thorns. Instead of a throne, Jesus was raised up on a cross. Instead of being anointed with oil, he was beaten. Instead of a rich, sumptuous feast, he was offered vinegar. Those nearby did not bow and scrape in this king's presence. Instead, they jeered. When we pray, "your kingdom come," do we realize we are praying for humility instead of greatness, for faithfulness even in the face of persecution, for a kingdom where God is revealed in suffering and brokenness?

God's Kingdom *Comes*

We pray, "your kingdom *come*." We ask for it, want it, expect it. This is anticipation of something we might have glimpsed, but is not yet complete. Luther put it this way in the Large Catechism: "The coming of God's kingdom to us takes place in two ways: first it comes here, in time, through the Word and faith, and second, in eternity, it comes through the final revelation. Now we ask for both of those things: that it may come to those who are not yet in it and that, by daily growth here and in eternal life hereafter, it may come to us who have attained it."[1]

To pray, "your kingdom *come*," shows vision and hope among those who pray. It is akin to praying, "Come, Holy Spirit." We know the Spirit came and was present when Jesus was baptized: "In those days Jesus came from Nazareth of Galilee and was baptized by John in the Jordan. And just as he was coming up out of the water, he saw the heavens torn apart and the Spirit descending like a dove on him" (Mark 1:9-10). We know the Spirit came and was present at Pentecost in a dramatic, unforgettable way: "And suddenly there came from heaven a sound like the rush of a violent wind, and it filled the entire house where they were sitting. Divided tongues, as of fire, appeared among them and a tongue rested on each of them. All of them were filled with the Holy Spirit and began to speak in other languages, as the Spirit gave them ability" (Acts 2:2-4). And yet we still pray, "Come, Holy Spirit." We know the Spirit has come, yet we pray for the Spirit to draw near in the moment and become obvious. We know that God's kingdom is among us; the kingdom of God is near. Still we pray that it come near us; we pray that its coming be fulfilled.

Considering the Kingdom in our Decisions

When we pray, "your kingdom come," we pray for a kingdom that draws near in the person of Jesus Christ and the evangelists he sends in pairs. We pray for a kingdom that is our treasure, that is inclusive, that elevates children to the highest position. So what does it mean to pray this at the crossroads of a decision? When trying to discern the right direction, this petition invites us to consider again who is in charge. It challenges us to turn from our selfishness, to turn from ourselves and turn to the King. It points us away from all we might treasure, to the reality that the kingdom itself is our greatest treasure. It reminds us that greatness is found in the least of these.

The challenge exists for all levels of decision makers, from the corporate office to the church councils to us as individuals. If a decision glorifies a company, a boss, or a volunteer, and does not point to God, can it really be the answer to "your kingdom come"? A Christian school in Chicago was facing tough times, and the board of trustees gave the mandate to balance the budget. Employees were let go with no notice. The mandate was met, but was God's kingdom reflected in the decision? If a decision elevates a group, a ministry, or an outreach, but does so at the expense of children, can it really be the answer to "your kingdom come"? A small congregation was approached by a crowded public school. Would the congregation rent their building to the school for considerable income? It looked like a great option at first, until leaders realized that two children's ministries and a seniors group would no longer be able to continue. The congregation declined the offer. If your decision turns your job, your schedule, your possessions or bank account into your god, if it is your top priority and your source of comfort, it cannot be God's answer to "your kingdom come."

On the other hand, if this prayer becomes action, then the decision would be one that honors the poor, not tramples them. The decision would honor the lost ones and bring them back. The decision would be one that allows us to worship and honor God, not hide our faith. If a decision reflects God's kingdom, it reflects a just and righteous world, a cared-for cosmos that was declared good. If a decision reflects God's kingdom, then humanity steps back into the God-given role as caretaker, not king or boss. Humans resume the role of caretaker for each other, for other creatures, and for creation itself. If a decision reflects God's kingdom, then God is in charge, children are honored, and others are invited to share in the kingdom.

Connecting with God's Word

Read Revelation 21:1-7. In this passage, John described a "new heaven" and a "new earth." The description is not one of tangible attributes, but rather a reality where God is among mortals. God is with them, and in this kingdom there is no death or crying or pain. What was your earliest understanding or mental picture of the word *kingdom*? How does this passage shift or deepen your understanding?

Considering the Crossroads

1. Are you a follower or a leader? Are you more comfortable as the boss or the worker?
2. Over which area of your life do you experience the most control? What would it look like or be like if God was in charge of that area of your life?
3. Over which area of your life do you experience the least control? What would it be like to know that God is with you?
4. How does reflecting on Jesus' humble kingship affect how you pray this petition? Does humility figure in your decision making? How would following Jesus' model of sacrifice help you as you stand at the crossroads?
5. What's the first step for you in giving up the micromanagement of a decision and praying for God's kingdom to come?

Your will be done. . . .

5

The Heart of the Prayer

One day he was on the layoff list, the next day he was safe. Day three he was on the list; on the final day when layoffs were announced, his job was spared. My husband's firm had been sold and in a drastic cost-cutting effort, seventy people had to go. John would have been number seventy-one. Though he didn't lose his job, his work group was reduced from twelve to four, deadlines were shortened, and he was asked to pick up the slack. Excellent workers were laid off; now they were disappearing as regularly and predictably (though not as quietly) as morning fog on a lake. John had a decision to make. Should he leave the industry? Should we leave the region we had called home for better options elsewhere? Talk about a need for discernment!

In the midst of the chaos and confusion, quite often there is no clear or simple choice between A and B. On the one hand, we debate employment stability and income versus children in school. On the other hand, we consider the opportunity for contentment and advancement versus beloved colleagues and fear of the unknown. To a large extent, the act of inviting God into a decision-making process, the act of discernment, rests on praying this petition: "Your will be done."

Distinguishing God's Will: Some Biblical Models

When we pray, "your will be done," are we not attempting to distinguish God's will from our desire, God's plan from our fervent wish? That's easier said than done. We may not feel adequate to discern God's will. Who are we to know the purposes of God? Thankfully, we have some guidance from God's Word. Our role models come from two powerful and poignant stories in the Bible. First, in Genesis, we read how God instructed Abraham to take his beloved son Isaac and offer him as a burnt offering on a mountain that God would point out. How, we might ask, would God make God's wishes known? Would any parents in their right minds willingly kill their son? Can we imagine a parent wishing for such a command? Obviously Abraham didn't have a problem with it, for we read, "When they came to the place that God had shown him, Abraham built an altar there and laid the wood in order. He bound his son Isaac and laid him on the altar, on top of the wood" (Gen. 22:9). Abraham obeyed God's command. But when Abraham raised his hand to kill his only son, an angel of the Lord called out and stopped him. Isaac was spared and a ram was sacrificed instead. And Abraham was told by the angel that because he did not withhold his own son, Abraham would be blessed.

Our second example comes from the Gospel of Luke, where it is recorded that after God's beloved Son shared the Passover with his followers, they went to the Mount of Olives, where Jesus withdrew from them to pray. "Father, if you are willing, remove this cup from me; yet, not my will but yours be done" (Luke 22:42), our Lord entreated. Shortly afterward, Jesus was arrested and tried. He was crucified and died between two convicted criminals. In this story, no angel intervened. No one kept the beloved Son from being killed. And in his hour of agony, wishing that the cup of suffering would not be his, he offered the future, his future, to his Father's will.

When we pray, "your will be done," do we mean it? Can we really put aside our ideas of what is best, what is safe, what is possible, and leave the situation in God's hands? Even if God's will is not what we would pick? It is not easy. Orson never wanted a viewing when he died. His nephew knew it. His friends knew it. His pastor knew it. So when the time came, despite questions and complaints, Orson's wishes were honored. They were honored by his family members and friends, who disagreed with the decision and longed to overrule him. Out of their love and respect for Orson, they put aside their own desires. But it wasn't easy.

One summer, I worked as a student chaplain at a medical center. My assignment was to minister in a handful of intensive care units. On one particular evening, family and extended family were crowded into a small meditation room. Because their prayers and tears were becoming louder and louder, the nurse had called for the student chaplain. The nurse in charge told me that the teenage patient had been arguing with a family member and had fallen off a balcony; he was not expected to live. When I arrived in the meditation room, an aunt grabbed my hand. "Pray with us, Chaplain! Pray our boy is okay and well and normal again. Pray that he is fine and will go home with us." Another member began to pray: "God, we know you have the power to heal. Jesus touched and restored many to complete health. We believe that miracles happen every day. Send us a miracle, Lord!" When the room was silent, I led the family in the Lord's Prayer. I stammered through it, unsure if I had met the family's request, but quite sure that God grants wholeness through death, and not just through wellness. The young man died late that night, and the student chaplain was there again, as family members yelled and wailed and lamented to God.

On Earth as in Heaven

This petition does not read "your will be done in heaven as it is on earth." Of course not. But we live, talk, and act like it does. Too often when we pray this petition we are ready, willing, and able to tell God exactly what God's will is, thank you very much! "Show us where to go, but please, God, keep us close to home." "Help us use the talents you give us, but please let it be in this three-county area." We have it backwards. The petition, of course, reads, "your will be done on earth *as in heaven.*"

So what is it like on earth? On earth, the beautiful are honored and the rich are revered. On earth, those who have, extend their credit and those who do not, receive welfare and are ostracized. On earth, the military has power, and heroes are those who are the fastest or strongest or are the best singers or dancers. On earth, God seems light-years away but everyone can buy their own phone and conduct business over lunch. On earth, the Sabbath is time for sleep, breakfast in bed, and youth sports. On earth, money buys happiness in the form of stuff that causes stress that sends us to the doctor that, in the end, requires more money. But heaven is different.

The pattern, played out again and again in the New Testament, is that heaven is not what we would expect; rather, it is often the opposite. In heaven the net is wide (Matt. 13:47). The poor are there, not the rich and satisfied (Luke 1:52-53). The lost are there and the wanderer is celebrated (Luke 15). In heaven, all creatures worship God all the time, twenty-four hours a day, seven days a week, and the lamb is on the throne (Rev. 4:8-11; 5:13). The lamb. Not the boss or spouse. Not the pastor or council president. Not the president of a country or a diplomat. The lamb—Jesus Christ—is on the throne. In heaven there is no pain or mourning. There is no darkness, no lock on the gate, and God is among the people (Revelation 21).

Not Praying for the Easy Answers

If we seriously pray, "your will be done on earth *as in heaven*," we are praying not for answers that increase our riches, our honor, or our recognition. We are praying for answers that recognize God blesses the poor and the meek. (Check out the Beatitudes in Luke 6.) We will pray for a decision that may not offer an easy out or an easy answer, but one that reflects an acceptance and comfort level with what is to come, as tough as it might be. When we pray, "your will be done on earth as in heaven," we pray in the spirit of Mary the Mother of our Lord. When Mary learned she was pregnant before she was married (scholars widely believe she was only a young teenager), there were many ways she could have responded, many tones she could have taken as she prayed. Would we, today, under the same circumstances have responded as she did? "My soul magnifies the Lord and my spirit rejoices in God my Savior, for he has looked with favor on the lowliness of his servant," sang Mary (Luke 1:46b-48). Mary did not pray for Joseph or her parents or her town to understand. She did not pray to be spared. She prayed, out of a sense of joy, *despite* the pain, sacrifice, and risk to come. We know that her story and the story of her Son were not pain-free. We know she still faced the pain of travel late in pregnancy, the pain of childbirth without technology and a bed. We know she still faced a fearful trip to Egypt so her young son would not be killed.

When we pray, "your will be done on earth as in heaven," Luther would say we are praying to keep the devil at bay at the same time we are praying in a way that will bring attack. This may seem foreign to our post-Enlightenment ears, but to Luther, the devil was real and opposed to everything good. In the Large Catechism, Luther wrote:

> If we try to hold these treasures (gospel, faith, Holy Spirit) fast, we will have to suffer an astonishing number of attacks and assaults from all who venture to hinder and thwart the fulfillment of the first two petitions. For no one can believe how the devil opposes and obstructs their fulfillment. He cannot bear to have anyone teach or behave rightly. Therefore, there is just as much need here as in every other case to ask without ceasing. Dear Father, your will be done and not the will of the devil or of our enemies, nor of those who would persecute and suppress your holy Word or prevent your kingdom from coming.[1]

We Lutherans acknowledge the existence and power of the devil, and it is reflected in our baptism service. Before baptizing in the name of the Father and of the Son and of the Holy Spirit, we first invite parents and sponsors (or the candidate, if an adult) to renounce the forces of evil, the devil and all his empty promises. God's will on earth as in heaven is a will that stands directly opposed to the devil, directly opposed to evil.

"Your will be done, on earth as in heaven." We live in the crossroads of this statement. We live in this world, on this earth, with an eye toward eternity. But the kingdom has not been fulfilled. We live in the in-between. And that is exactly where we find ourselves when faced with a difficult decision, when living through transition, when trying to discern God's will. In those moments, we are at a crossroads. My husband spent the better part of a year sending resumes to every newspaper, every firm he could think of. Resumes blanketed the east coast from upstate New York to North Carolina, and one almost made its way to Arkansas. Ultimately, a solid, respected firm in the Philly area hired him, and he began a new job with considerable more job security for less pay. You face two choices, two possible directions (or maybe more, maybe your crossroads is a five-point intersection!). At that intersection you can see signs and signals, but you cannot see the entire road and you certainly cannot see the end it. At the crossroads of the decision, at the crossroads between heaven and earth we pray, "your will be done on earth as in heaven."

Connecting with God's Word

Read Luke 22:39-45. This passage finds Jesus on the Mount of Olives before his arrest and trial, praying to his Father. It is honest; Jesus asks that he be spared. But it is selfless; Jesus prays (not when his suffering has ended and he has risen, but in the midst of his angst) "not my will but yours be done." How do your prayers change depending on your stress-level or depending on where you are in the decision-making process?

Considering the Crossroads

1. On what issues are you least likely to compromise? Why? What is at stake?
2. What is the most recent situation about which you prayed for a particular result? How did the outcome impact your faith?
3. A colleague calls praying for (or dictating) specific results, "vending machine prayers." We approach God and try to pick a specific answer like we would pick a snack. How does this type of prayer compare and contrast to praying, "your will be done?" Which is easier to pray and why?
4. In what ways are you prepared (or ill-prepared) to accept an answer to your prayer? What if God's will is not what you wish?

Give us today our daily bread. . . .

6

Perpetual Potluck

Our sweet canine, Molly, has issues, which I guess is true of many dogs adopted from the ASPCA. She came to us without a complete history, but we do know that she was taken to the ASPCA several days after her original owner died. She did not know how to play. She did not trust the security we offered. Molly lives each day as if she will never eat again. Eight years after her adoption, I still find wrapped fortune cookies deep in the chairs and hidden under the cushion of her bed. I find a squeaky-clean plastic lid in the middle of the floor. Or, my favorite memory: finding three petrified hamburger buns, still in the bag, wedged back in a corner under the radiator. The only time Molly has ever been in a dogfight, she was defending the grease drip pan under the grill.

Trusting Means Freedom from Fear

The sad truth is many faithful believers with abundant blessings live their daily lives like Molly does. These scared humans hide and hoard, worried that what they have will not last or is not enough. They save for a rainy day, not trusting that God truly provides today the bread we need for tomorrow. Individuals monitor stocks, move accounts for better interest, and, when things are tight, cut charitable giving. It not only happens at the individual level. Even churches can fall victim to fear; congregations often see what is lacking and not the abundant blessings around them. Finance committees guard the endowment, afraid of tomorrow, protecting assets in case of hard times. For those who grew up in the era of The Great Depression, such an outlook might be understandable. If you have lived through uncertainty, scarcity, and economic hardship, you save and prepare and hide resources away. The danger today is that if we Christians live like it is still 1932, we will miss opportunities for blessing; we will not see opportunities to be the church right before our eyes. And if we long for the heyday of the 1950s, we miss today.

It happens in families as well. After months of uncertainty and the pursuit of other options, Kevin decided to retire. After thirty years in one field, he left the workplace to pursue non-work interests. Had Kevin worked ten more years, his pension would have almost equaled his last salary and provided him with more security. Instead, Kevin retired early, and now he volunteers at the senior center, babysits his grandchildren, and has experienced a drop in his blood pressure. No clear-cut, hands-down obvious choice. He could have held tight to what was comfortable, what was familiar. But holding on might have led to despair, which might lead to the inability to make a change. What comes first? Angst or refusal to change? Can we see the abundance of retirement in the midst of the uncertainty of leaving the familiar workplace?

That precisely is the challenge. To keep in our sights the reality of the abundant blessings in our lives—life itself, shelter, food, clothing— while we wrestle with the moments of lack. Martha was balancing her checkbook, wondering how she was going to meet expenses now that Reuben had died. Martha confided in her best friend that she probably would need to stop donating to her church and other charities. Could she still pay tuition for her son? Could she still afford her medications? Martha's best friend reminded her of the pension that would soon come in, the grants available for tuition, and the blessing of having already paid off the mortgage. Martha gradually made the adjustments and continued as a faithful giver to her church. Six months after her first conversation about financial fears, she was offered a new job paying twenty percent more. As a result, she even increased her charitable donations.

Recognizing the Blessings

I believe that focusing on scarcity triggers within us the fear that causes us to cling so tightly to what is, that we cannot let go to grab what might be. In fact, some of us spend so much time complaining about what we don't have and what we want that we do not realize the blessings that surround us. This is nothing new. The people of God have never seemed satisfied with what God provides. We only have to look back to Moses to see that.

Jesus' hearers were familiar with the history of God's people. They could recount how the Israelites complained bitterly to Moses and Aaron in the wilderness, "If only we had died by the hand of the Lord in Egypt. . . for you have brought us out into this wilderness to kill this whole assembly with hunger" (Exod. 16:3). We too, remember the story, but it seems a little silly to us. Who were they kidding? Didn't they remember Pharaoh, who forced them into slavery? Anything would be better than their life in Egypt, right? Our reaction is perhaps couched in the knowledge that God did not forget the Chosen People in the wilderness. Despite their seeming ingratitude, God responded immediately and directly. God rained bread from heaven and instructed the people to go and gather just enough for one day. "Morning by morning they gathered it; as much as each needed" (Exod. 16:21). It was, quite literally, daily bread for the Israelites in the wilderness. The crisis was solved, until they ran low on water and the complaining began anew. Finally Moses himself complained to God—not about food, but about the people! "What shall I do with this people? They are almost ready to stone me" (Exod. 17:4).

And so it went. Complaint; provision from God. More complaining, more provision. But of what had they lost sight? They no longer were in slavery; they no longer were under Pharaoh's thumb. They were free. And they had bread (manna) for the day and water for the day— both pure gifts from God. But did they give thanks? Hardly. What about us? Do we give thanks for the abundant blessings or complain about what is missing? A friend described his weariness after Easter services. As pastor, he had welcomed back families who had been gone for awhile; he had welcomed neighbors who had never before attended; he had welcomed extended family members of congregants. On her way out the door, a member shook his hand and greeted him with, "Pastor, isn't a shame that the pews are not filled and we no longer need three services like we used to?"

How we view the world, in fact how we view the reality of our circumstances, can assist us in the discernment process or stop us in our tracks. If your family is struggling, and you question whether you can make ends meet, discerning God's will is centered on how to provide food for your family just for tonight. You do not have the luxury of contemplating the bigger picture until the daily bread is provided. Your questions will not likely be: What job best fits my talents? If I went back to school would it ultimately help the family or society at large? On the other hand, if you have inherited money and have never wanted for anything, do you dare explore how you use your resources? Or do you hide, hoard, and protect, like my dog Molly? Might there be opportunity to share your wealth and in so doing, make a difference in the world? Sharing requires faith, resources, and energy. Sharing is a hint that we have hope in tomorrow and perhaps even a vision of a better day.

Praying for More than Bread

When Martin Luther discussed this petition of the Lord's Prayer, he went beyond thinking of daily bread as financial resources. To him, daily bread included everything involved in getting a meal on the table. In the Large Catechism, Luther wrote: "You must therefore expand and extend your thoughts to include not just the oven or the flour bin, but also the broad fields and the whole land that produce and provide our daily bread and all kinds of sustenance for us. For if God did not cause grain to grow and did not bless it and preserve it in the field, we could never have a loaf of bread to take from the oven or set upon the table."[1]

In today's world, then, praying for our daily bread includes praying for the earth, and, as with other prayers, putting our prayers in action. How might you reduce your dependence on gasoline? How environmentally friendly is your home? Do you recycle, regulate your thermostat to conserve, and use energy-efficient light bulbs? As we pray for our daily bread, we connect in prayer with Christians across the world who walk miles each day for water. Our prayer, put into action, might provide daily bread for another.

When you pray, "give us this day our daily bread," how often is your next thought a prayer for the government? As Luther discussed this petition, he went in an amazing direction, recognizing that an instable government takes daily bread from the mouths of citizens:

Indeed, the greatest need of all is to pray for the civil authorities and government, for it is chiefly through them that God provides us daily bread and all the comforts of this life. Although we have received from God all good things in abundance, we cannot retain any of them or enjoy them in security and happiness were he not to give us a stable, peaceful government. For where dissension, strife, and war prevail, there daily bread is already taken away or at least reduced.[2]

It is not a stretch then to realize that praying "give us this day our daily bread" is also a prayer not just for our government but for the governments and nations of the world. We pray for peace, that God's children in every land will have access to daily bread.

Being Faithful with What We Are Given

So what about your circumstance, your individual crossroads? Perhaps you feel you are traversing the desert, wondering if the water has run out. Perhaps you are a senior on a fixed income having to choose which prescribed medications you can take and which you ignore based on your income. Perhaps you are approaching middle age, wondering how you will balance mortgage, car payments, and your child's college tuition. Perhaps you are a young adult about to start your first job and realizing the income does not quite cover expenses. What you decide at the crossroads is connected to how you view the scenery. It can look vast and empty, and all you see is what is lacking. Or it can look expansive and promising, with a myriad of opportunities ahead.

Jesus told a parable. We call it the parable of the talents. You can read it in Luke 19. It seems a guy traveled internationally to gain power; he summoned ten workers before he left and gave them each one talent or pound (believed to be the eqivalent of three-months' wages). When the business guru returned from his overseas travel, he called his workers to give an accounting. The first had taken one and made it ten. The second took one and made it five. Both were praised. The third was afraid; he had heard the boss was a tough guy, a harsh supervisor. The third hid the one and returned it. We don't even know what happened to the other seven workers. The parable ends with the boss's wrath; he gives the one portion to the guy with the most. We are called to be faithful with what we are given—not just financial resources but also with time and ability. What we have varies from person to person, but God asks that we not waste what we have. Back in the wilderness with Moses, the day the people left manna on the ground figuring they'd collect it the next morning, they awoke to find the manna had rotted and was overcome with worms (Exod. 16:20). Give us this day our *daily* bread.

Connecting with God's Word

Read John 6:22-35. This passage follows the story where Jesus fed the crowd with five loaves and two fish. In these verses, Jesus encourages the people to concern themselves not with food that perishes but with what feeds them forever. He tells them that he is the bread of life. Just as their ancestors were fed with manna from heaven, "I am the bread that came down from heaven" (v. 41). How do Jesus' words comfort (or challenge you) as you pray for daily bread?

Considering the Crossroads

1. What is the hardest thing (person, issue) to entrust to God? Why?
2. How does your trust (or lack of trust) in God impact your decision-making?
3. How do your choices on this pending decision impact others? In particular, how do your choices affect the ability of others in your family or community to access their daily bread?
4. What do you think is the role of the church in providing daily bread? What opportunities for blessing do we as followers of Christ have to offer those who stand at the crossroads?

Forgive us our sins, as we forgive. . . .

7

Let Go to Lighten the Load

It had been a perfect autumn day in seminary, the kind of day when remaining cooped up in class was painful. I was more than ready to relax in the privacy of the old-house apartment I called home. A major paper and project on the topic of the Lord's Prayer for toddlers were due the next day. The project was done; the paper required a few more pages and some editing. It would be completed early at this rate, and I could relax. My boys, ages three and eight, were enjoying the crisp fall air, complete with jumping in leaf piles. Dinner, bath, story. Sometime between their bedtime and my bedtime, I was at work at the computer, finishing my paper, when toddler Thomas wandered into the room, bleary eyed, needing water or a hug. As I turned to hug him, he turned the other way, asked, "What is this?" and hit a series of computer keys. The paper was gone. Obliterated, not just deleted. At the moment, I could not see the irony and humor; I was working on something for a child who was roughly the same age as Luther's son, Hans, when Luther wrote the catechism. Only now I can envision Hans asking the same question again and again: "What is this?"

Dejected, panicked, overwhelmed, and angry, I sat staring at the computer, saying "no, no, no" over and over. I called one classmate to babysit and another to ask if I could come over. After venting and pounding a cinderblock wall, I returned home to find Thomas was tucked snugly in bed. In the quiet calm, I recreated the paper. Before heading to bed in the wee hours of the morning, I went in to Thomas, rubbed his head lightly, kissed his cheek, and said, "I love you." I forgave Thomas and headed to bed feeling free: free from frustration as well as free to ask God to forgive me for being angry in the first place. I am still living into the realization that I pray for conditional forgiveness. Forgive me my sins, *as* I forgive those who sin against me.

Attempting the Impossible?

When Peter asked Jesus how many times he should forgive, the outer limits he could imagine was seven times. Instead, Jesus told Peter to forgive seventy-seven times (Matt. 18:21-22). The number seven was known to be the number of completion; some say perfection. It seems that would be enough forgiveness. But instead, Jesus gave an even higher, unimaginable number. How many times should we forgive? There is no limit. We are to forgive endlessly, forever, over and over. So what stops us? What keeps us from forgiving the first time, much less the seventh or the seventy-seventh time? Perhaps it is the depth of our anger or hurt. Perhaps it is the number of times the same person has violated our trust. Perhaps the resentment has become habit. Perhaps we are waiting for a proper apology.

It is easy to look at this petition as an impossible task. We may wish we could forgive, but we just cannot seem to bring ourselves to do it. In the Large Catechism, Luther challenged believers to see the grace in this petition: "This petition really means that God does not wish to regard our sins and punish us as we daily deserve but to deal graciously with us, to forgive us as he has promised, and thus to grant us a joyful and cheerful conscience so that we may stand before him in prayer."[1] But there is a challenge. Much as we might want to ignore the second phrase, the petition does not end with "Forgive us our sins." Rather, it continues: ". . . as we forgive those who sin against us." According to Luther, in this second part, God "has promised us assurance that everything is forgiven and pardoned, yet on the condition that we also forgive our neighbor."[2]

Many years ago I attended a weeklong Bible conference for adolescents. The featured young preacher chose the text from Matthew that numerous church bodies turn to on issues of discipline, forgiveness, and reconciliation. Here's a quick summary: If you have something against your brother first go alone to the other person; if needed then take one or two others with you. Finally, tell it to the church and if there is no reconciliation, then the sinner will be to you like an outcast (Matt. 18:15-20). The message was powerful and memorable. It was also contrary to everything my adolescent mind could comprehend about forgiveness and reconciliation. My world revolved around fairness. I believed I was supposed to forgive someone who wronged me only *if* and *after* they apologized. My forgiveness was the reward for their feeling contrite, admitting wrong, and asking for my forgiveness. But no, the sermon made a different point quite clearly: the one who *has been wronged* is to take responsibility for reconciliation. The one who is hurt takes the first step to make things right again, even if the one who was sinned against never gets an apology.

All these years later I still remember the message. Why? Because it is contrary to what we expect; it goes against our human nature. We are programmed to forgive someone *after* they apologize, not *before*. We expect that if someone has wronged us, they will say they are sorry; likewise if someone apologizes to us, we are expected to forgive them. This sermon stuck with me because I was encouraged to let go, to forgive without ever receiving an apology—to forgive even if the other person never realized the hurt he or she caused. The sermon did not grant a "pass" based on the depth of my hurt or anger. And the scripture does not release me from forgiving someone even if it is the same person who has hurt me for the seventh time in the exact same way. If you hurt me, I come to you to make it right again. I might think my forgiving you frees you from the guilt and shame of doing something wrong. In reality, it frees *me*—from ulcers, depression, or whatever other maladies repressed anger can bring about. Thirty-four years later the message is still powerful and still challenging.

Forgiven to Live Freely

It is important to say that receiving forgiveness does not free us from the civil consequences of our actions. A while back, I saw a news account of a woman who forgave a drunk driver for killing her child in a car crash. Though forgiven by the victim's family, the driver was still charged and served time for the offense. Absolution doesn't mean we are exempt from judgment. We still have to own up to what we have done wrong and face what we deserve. Forgiveness doesn't erase all that has taken place. It does, however, give hope for a different outcome, a different future, a renewed relationship. Neither do I mean to imply that forgiveness is easy or cheap. In my own experience, resentment and anger often create and strengthen a barrier between me and the person with whom I am angry. I become stuck in the conflict. It is as if resentment is quicksand, and every motion, every attempt to physically release the anger causes me to sink deeper and become more seriously stuck. Forgiveness is the lifeline that enables me to be released and free.

Julie and Mac were trying to decide whether to have children. They knew there would be doctor's visits, check-ups, and official word on the status of their health. But in the meantime, they were considering the decision from other angles too. Could they afford the cost of formula, clothes, and other expenses if one of them quit work to stay home? Could they afford childcare? Given their relationships with their own parents, did they *want* to be parents? Julie remembered clearly her harsh father and timid mother. She spent years resenting the beatings she received, and she was angry that her mother never stood up for her. In the midst of that anger and resentment, making a decision about having children of her own seemed impossible for Julie. But in this case, through counseling, Julie gradually let go of the past and is no longer stuck in her anger. She is now considering parenting based on her individual strengths and love of children. Letting go freed her to make a clear decision.

For years, Pat's in-laws had ignored his birthday. His curiosity led to resentment, which led to anger. When Pat turned fifty, his father-in-law was hospitalized. After the man was released from the hospital, Pat paid him a visit. They shared memories of fishing and golfing together. They even laughed. Finally Pat admitted he had been hurt by the neglect. His father-in-law got teary-eyed, admitted to never being good with dates, and promptly wrote the date of Pat's birthday on his calendar. When Pat turned fifty-one, three generations gathered to celebrate, courtesy of his in-laws.

God forgives us before we pray, Martin Luther acknowledged. In the same way that God's name is holy and God's kingdom will come regardless of our prayer. So why pray? In the Large Catechism, Luther put it this way: "The point here is for us to recognize and accept this forgiveness. For the flesh in which we daily live is of such a nature that it does not trust and believe God and is constantly aroused by evil desires and devices, so that we sin daily in word and deed, in acts of commission and omission. Therefore it is necessary constantly to run to this petition and get the comfort that will restore our conscience."[3]

It is not easy, and we cannot expect it to be. This is not a quick fix with nothing expected of us in return. The prayer teaches, "Forgive us our sins as we forgive those who sin against us." According to Luther, "just as we sin greatly against God every day and yet he forgives it all through grace, so we also must always forgive our neighbor who does us harm, violence, and injustice, bears malice toward us."[4] So the question is, can you choose to forgive and move forward? As you stand at the crossroads, can you at least pray that God will forgive and help you let go?

After answering Peter's question about how often to forgive, Jesus told the story of a king who was to settle accounts with his slaves (Luke 18). The first owed the king 10,000 talents and could not pay. The consequences were that this slave and his family would be sold. When the slave begged for mercy, the king forgave the entire debt. Then the forgiven slave promptly went out and shook down another who owed him 100 denarii. The plea for mercy fell on deaf ears. But when the king found out, the slave was tortured. It is a vivid and dramatic story, one that drives home the connection between our being forgiven and our forgiving others.

We pray that God would forgive us as we forgive others. Forgive us for not having enough faith, for walking past someone in need. Forgive us for being lazy and complacent. Forgive us for complaining and seeing worry and lack rather than opportunity and abundance. And God does. But what if we do not believe we are forgiven? What if all this sounds nice, but we are not convinced it relates to us? As Lutherans we can find reassurance in our baptism. Not merely a dedication or a naming ceremony, the sacrament is God's promise to us (for many of us as infants) before we can begin to understand or claim the promise for ourselves. In the Small Catechism, Luther enumerated the benefits of baptism: "It brings about forgiveness of sins, redeems from death and the devil, and gives eternal salvation to all who believe it, as the Word and promise of God declare."[5] Forgiveness frees us. Frees us to explore new options. Frees us to share the good news of God's love. It frees us to think creatively about the future. Living in the past inhibits our ability to appreciate the present or look to the future; forgiveness moves us into a new relationship with God and others. With less old baggage to carry, we might be freer to explore what God has in mind for us.

Connecting with God's Word

Read John 21:15-19. Not too long before this conversation, Peter had vehemently denied knowing Jesus during a time when Jesus most needed the support of the twelve. Jesus had been arrested and was facing trial and crucifixion when, three times, Peter denied knowing him. In this passage, we see how after Jesus has risen, he came to Peter and restored the relationship three times, allowing Peter to declare his love of the Lord and reminding him of his role to care for others. How does Jesus' allowing Peter three times to declare his love free Peter to proclaim the risen Christ and continue to share the good news? How might the reality of God's forgiveness to you free you to make a decision that would honor God?

Considering the Crossroads

1. Is there something for which you cannot forgive yourself? What is it?
2. Whose portrait pops into your head when you hear the word *resentment*?
3. Can you believe that you are forgiven? How does your answer impact your discernment process?

Save us from the time of trial....

8

Toil and Turmoil

My husband John was on the way home from the store when a radio news account sent chills down his spine. A local five-year-old kindergarten student had died in a school accident. Our Thomas was five at the time; he was in kindergarten at the mentioned school. John drove home in a mental fog. For fifteen gut-wrenching minutes he feared our youngest son was dead. It was not Thomas, but a classmate, a young towhead with all the energy and exuberance of Curious George.[1] He was a boy from the neighborhood with whom I interacted while volunteering in the classroom. His smile could melt butter, and everyone loved him. One morning his mother sent him to school and he did not return. Four months after my ordination, I led a kindergarten-appropriate memorial service for the family, the child's classmates, and the school staff—a task I could never have imagined would be a part of my ministry. John's fifteen-minute ride home; my days of sitting with grieving children and working with school psychologists and leading a memorial for Thomas' friend; the never-ending grief—they remain some of the darkest days of my life.

Struggling to Make Sense of Tragedy

I am not sure it is possible to make complete sense of a tragedy such as the one that befell the boy's family and community. Most attempts seem cliché or seem to trivialize the depth of the pain. The question really boils down to God's role in suffering. Could God have prevented the death? Is the death punishment? Do the eventual improvements in safety ever balance the tragic loss of young life? How dare we continue to pray, "save us from the time of trial," when seemingly random and obviously tragic losses occur all the time. Perhaps we continue to pray because in faith we cling to the reality that God is with us no matter what life dishes out. Perhaps we continue to pray because we need some place to which we can turn and someone on whom we can lean, instead of lashing out in anger. While we may not escape a tragic event in life, perhaps we pray that we might be saved from the consequences of taking justice into our own hands.

In times of trial, we look for a scapegoat; we seek an outlet for the anger, grief, and anguish. In biblical times, the scapegoat was not a metaphor. A goat would be sent into the wilderness and left alone until it died; it was thought that the goat's death would be a sacrifice for the sins of all in the village. While we seek outlets for our anguish, we should take care not to just dump them on someone else. In the darkest times of life we are tempted to lean on Hebraic law: "Anyone who maims another shall suffer the same injury in return: fracture for fracture, eye for eye, tooth for tooth; the injury inflicted is the injury to be suffered" (Lev. 24:19-20). Jesus, well versed in Jewish law, quoted the law but then rewrote it for the future: "You have heard that it was said, 'An eye for an eye and a tooth for a tooth.' But I say to you, Do not resist an evildoer. But if anyone strikes you on the right cheek, turn the other also; and if anyone wants to sue you and take your coat, give your cloak as well; and if anyone forces you to go one mile, go also the second mile" (Matt. 5:38-41). We are not to seek revenge, but instead to take extra means to help and be kind to the one who would harm us.

I dare say that our overwhelming preference would be to adhere to Levitical guidelines. If I am wronged, I take revenge in kind. If someone hurts me, I hurt them in the same way, thus equaling the score. I think it may be our human nature to respond this way, given my observation of schoolyard fights! The teaching of Jesus, to turn the other cheek, to give up your coat, was counter cultural then and is countercultural now. We are wronged, so we sue; we are angry, so we lash out; we are hurt, so we hurt someone else. Sometimes we even become our own scapegoat by accepting blame for someone else's situation, by trying to drown guilt in alcohol, and by turning our anger inward. Too often we are the target of our own anger and anguish. It comes in the form of guilt: "If only I had kept him home. If only I had asked more questions, paid more attention, or done things differently." Whether it is desire for revenge or whether it is deep guilt or something else altogether, each gets in the way of discerning God's will; each keeps us from making a clear choice. Blinded by emotion, it becomes impossible to see the path in front of us, as if our emotions were a thick fog rolling in across the road.

Facing Temptation

No sooner did Jesus rise from the baptismal waters of the Jordan, than he was led by the Holy Spirit into the wilderness (Matt. 4:1-11). For forty days he fasted, and at the end of that fast, Jesus was greeted by the devil. Three times the devil tempted Jesus. Knowing that Jesus was hungry, the devil tempted him to change stones into bread. Knowing that the wilderness was a dangerous place that made humans vulnerable, the devil tempted Jesus to jump off a cliff and let the angels protect him. And last but not least, the devil tempted Jesus by offering him all the land as far as the eye could see, if only Jesus would bow and worship the devil.

The same temptations face us today. We are tempted to make poor choices when we lack necessities. News stories tell of parents stealing to feed their children, of young adults killing each other for a jacket. We are tempted to make questionable choices for the sake of safety and security. We might move to the safety of a better neighborhood but in the process deny our child an education. We are tempted to choose in order to ensure our success, to accumulate more money, more possessions, more respect, and more authority. A college graduate might look only at the starting salary and not realize that the firm exploits its workers. A teacher might be tempted to give up the job at the small public school where every encounter makes a difference, for the higher income at a large private school where the experience is a great line on the resume. The choices are not easy and the right option is not always clear-cut. Jesus leaves us with the word of God as our help during temptation. Luther admits that we come to this petition as forgiven people, "yet such is life that one stands today and falls tomorrow."[2]

Luther's Understanding

When we pray "save us from the time of trial," we do not pray to be spared, but rather we pray that God does not lead us in the direction of temptation. As Luther put it, "We do not say, 'Spare us the trial,' but 'Do not lead us into it.' It is as if we were to say, 'We are surrounded on all sides by trials and cannot avoid them; however, dear Father, help us so that we do not fall prey to them and yield to them, and thus be overcome and vanquished.'"[3]

Luther divided temptation into three categories: flesh, world, and the devil. Each was at the root of the temptations Jesus experienced in the Matthew account. The first, to change stones to food, was a temptation of the flesh that is the human body. The second, to throw himself off a cliff and let the angels catch him, was another temptation of the flesh. The third, to worship the devil, thereby gaining worldly power and possessions, was a temptation concerning the world and the devil. All of course, were temptations posed by the devil himself. In the Large Catechism, Luther suggested that the flesh is our sinful nature which "goes to work and lures us into unchastity, laziness, gluttony and drunkenness, greed and deceit, into acts of defraud and deception against our neighbor."[4] The world, he wrote, leads to anger and impatience. In this worldly category of temptation, we find violence, injustice, vengeance, cursing, slander, pride, and more. The devil would "tear us away from faith, hope and love, to draw us into disbelief, false security and stubbornness, or on the contrary, to drive us into despair, denial of God and countless other abominable sins."[5] Throughout our lives as believers, we are under constant attack from the devil, he said.

> This, then is what "leading us not into temptation" means: when God gives us power and strength to resist, even though the attack is not removed or ended. For no one can escape temptations and allurements as long as we live in the flesh and have the devil prowling around us. We cannot help but suffer attacks, and even be moored in them, but we pray here that we may not fall into them and be drowned by them. . . .

At such times our only help and comfort is to run here and seize hold of the Lord's Prayer and to speak to God from our heart, "Dear Father, you have commanded me to pray; let me not fall because of temptation."[6]

Temptation at the Crossroads

It is the nature of decision-making that it is often required during the most stressful of times. A loved one's care, a child's future, a choice in vocation, or some other important decision often hangs in the balance. The stress of making such a decision may seem so overwhelming that we just want to throw up our hands in surrender. We are vulnerable, which makes us easy targets for "have-I-got-an-offer-for-you" promises of ease and comfort. During vulnerable times, we can be targets for deceit. As a child, I thought my allowance was too low. So when Freddie needed a pencil and offered me a dollar, I jumped at the chance. Two days later when he offered me a dollar per sheet for paper, I thought I had found a gravy train. Our deals went on for a week or so until one night my parents asked me for the money. Seems Freddie had been stealing money from someone else to make me such great offers. The saying goes, "If it sounds too good to be true, it probably is." God promises to save us from despair. And being saved from the depths of that agony, perhaps we can see God in the midst of the pain or uncertainty. If we can sense that God is close to us during times of trial, we can more clearly consider the decisions that face us.

As you stand at the crossroads of a critical decision, it is helpful to think about what tempts you and why it is a temptation and in what manner you naturally respond. It is also helpful to consider the petition that we not be led into temptation. In a sense, we can find enough temptation on our own; please, God, spare us from being led into them as a test or trial. It is helpful to think of the trials in life and how we respond. If our decision is motivated by sinful desires, if it is motivated by power, fame, money, or authority, then could it really be God's will? Those are the options that Jesus himself rejected. If our decision paves the way for greed or deceit, if it fuels laziness or injustice or pride, if it leads another person into temptation, then we should think twice.

Connecting with God's Word

Read Matthew 4:1-11. The wilderness experience of Jesus immediately followed his baptism. To what extent do you agree or disagree with Luther, who says that baptism makes the devil our lifelong enemy?

Of the temptations Jesus faced, which stands in the way of your ability to move forward with a clear decision, and why? (The temptation over necessities, safety and security, or success and power?)

"Then Jesus was led up by the Spirit into the wilderness to be tempted by the devil" (v. 1). How does the realization that the Spirit led Jesus into the wilderness to be tempted impact the way you pray, "save us from the time of trial"?

Considering the Crossroads

1. Share a "time of trial" from your personal life or the life of your community. How did God seem present? How did God feel absent? How did this affect the decisions you made?
2. Who or what is the cause of suffering? How does your answer help you (or make it harder) to turn to God, to pray when you are at a crossroads facing a major decision?

Deliver us from evil. . . .

9

God, Have Mercy

An inner-city colleague tells this personal story of fright. A visitor attended her church for the first time one spring Sunday morning and asked immediately to join the congregation. Given the number of visitors that day and the customary warmth and welcome that the pastor and people offered, no one thought twice about the request. But when the visitor filled out a new member information form, a member questioned a few job experiences and realized the visitor was not entirely truthful about whom he claimed to be. He had lived nearby for years, yet no one knew him. Each week he sat with children in the church and gave them gifts. Neighbors saw him watching the church, rattling the gates, and the pastor recalled that he would phone the minute she returned from visitation with twenty questions about where she had been. He once came to the church office armed and bragged about his marksmanship. He brought a 100-pound dog to the office, introducing it as his lifelong companion. Some days he glorified the pastor, crediting her with the good in his life; other days he demonized her, blaming her for all the negative things that had happened to him. The prospective member emailed the pastor nearly eighty times in a month. His communications became more threatening, and the pastor feared for her safety. She even contemplated leaving the ministry.

Deciding in Fear

Fear, whether perceived or realized, makes it nearly impossible to make a serious and responsible decision. As humans, our typical response when threatened is to fight or run. We are at a stressful crossroads when confronted with that which is frightening to us. In the case of my colleague, a physical fight with the prospective member would have been pointless. But the temptation to run was probably premature too. Would it have been responsible to renounce the ministry without first going to the police or turning to the regional church office for advice and slowing the process of converting a visitor to a member? Probably not, but fear was the driving the force, not rational thinking.

We read about danger in the headlines every day. Sometimes the threat seems far away. Terrorist attacks. Global warming. Pandemics. Other times the danger is too close for comfort. In my own neighborhood, a teen was gunned down five blocks away, caught in the crossfire of a drug war. One of my young church members was brutally murdered, her body dumped in the woods. The headlines are not always anonymous, and the fear they evoke is very real.

"Deliver us from evil," we pray. Perhaps we might also add, "Deliver us from fear." We fear the unknown: the future, a stranger, a new job or school, a new home or church. The existence of evil in the world makes it worse. How many people fear flying now, who did not in 2000? How many people fear opening the mail now, who did not before we knew what anthrax was? Evil moments in the news—murder, terrorism, poisoning, torture—all fuel our fear. In virtually every community across our country, spouses suffer verbal or physical abuse. Each day they experience fear that too often keeps them in a dangerous situation. After all, there are often additional threats if the one in danger decides to leave. So they do nothing. Both evil and fear freeze us in our tracks; they render us unable to discern our next best step. "Deliver us from evil. Deliver us from fear." I think the prayers go hand in hand.

The power of fear is not relegated only to situations that are dangerous. The same crippling dynamics of fear are at work whenever we might be at a crossroads. As pastor, what would happen if, fearing money would run out, I proposed cutting benevolences, quit ordering curriculum, or held off on the next evangelism push? The church would be headed toward irrelevancy in the community. What if, as a student, you feared failure so much that you never took a class? What if a fear kept you from trying a new thing? You would miss out on opportunities and limit yourself. What if you feared conflict to the point that you avoided deep, healthy conversations—complete with disagreement—

that could lead to new vision, new energy, and new opportunities? What if you feared rising debt to the point that you allowed yourself to remain stuck in a job that did not satisfy?

We fear change. We fear the time, energy, and emotion that change requires. We fear it so much that we live our entire lives in the same zip code. We fear failure so much that we never explore a new opportunity. Some would argue that our reaction to fear is human nature, and some would say, a protective device. I believe that fear is the opposite of faith. Whether we fear an individual or a nation, whether we fear the changes around us or the lack of change we find in our own existence, fear is a form of turning in on ourselves. We shut others out, figuratively or literally, isolating ourselves thinking it will protect us. When we fear another person, we might cut off communication or even personal contact with the individual. When we fear a situation, even one that could bring joy, such as a crowd at a wedding reception, we pass on the event and isolate ourselves further. When we turn in on ourselves, it leaves little motivation to turn to God.

I also believe that God understands fear. Mary, an unmarried teenager, was visited by an angel who told her she would conceive and bear the Messiah. After initially greeting her and declaring her blessed, the angel's next words were, "Do not be afraid" (Luke 1:30). After asking some questions, Mary, free of fear, accepted the news and praised God. When shepherds were going about their jobs on the hillside, "An angel of the Lord stood before them, and the glory of the Lord shone around them, and they were terrified. But the angel said to them, 'Do not be afraid'" (Luke 2:9-10). After realizing the news was good, the shepherds were freed from fear and decided to go and see for themselves and worship the newborn Christ. When the women went to Jesus' tomb early one morning, the found the stone rolled away and an angel sitting on it. The angel's first words were, "Do not be afraid" (Matt. 28:5). After hearing the reassurance, seeing the empty tomb, they were able to share the news with others. Likewise it is possible for us, when experiencing the reassurance of God's loving presence, to accomplish things or witness things we once feared.

The Reality of Evil

"Deliver us from evil," we pray. Did you ever stop to realize that by praying this petition, we acknowledge the very existence of evil? It would make no sense, after all, to pray for deliverance from something that does not exist. We pray to be delivered from evil. We do not pray, "Deliver us from perceived threats." We do not pray, "Deliver us from hardship." The prayer is, "Deliver us from evil." Evil exists. We turn to God for deliverance.

Another possible reading of "evil" in the Lord's Prayer, if we return to the Greek, is "evil one." Deliver us from the evil one—the devil, Satan—present in scripture and renounced in Lutheran baptismal services, but often underestimated, ignored, or relegated to the status of an imaginary character. In a May 2007 Gallup poll, seventy percent of 1,003 adults surveyed in the United States said they believed in the devil. They did not say what form or idea the devil takes in their minds. Perhaps for some the devil is a red creature with horns and a pitchfork or a dark cloaked creature, akin to the grim reaper. It doesn't really matter. Do we really need to know what the devil looks like, any more than we need to know what God looks like, in order to believe?

In the Large Catechism, Luther wrote, "In the Greek this petition reads, 'Deliver or preserve us from the Evil One or the Wicked One.' It seems to be speaking of the devil as the sum of all evil in order that the entire substance of our prayer may be directed against our archenemy. For it is he who obstructs everything for which we ask: God's name or honor, God's kingdom and will, our daily bread, a good and cheerful conscience, etc."[1] Luther defined evil in terms of "poverty, disgrace, death, and, in short, all the tragic misery and heartache, of which there is so incalculably much on the earth," calling the devil both a liar and a murderer. According to Luther, the devil "incessantly seeks our life and vents his anger by causing accidents, and injury to our bodies. He crushes some and drives others to insanity; some he drowns in water, and many he hounds to suicide or other dreadful catastrophe."[2]

But there is hope for us. After all, if we belong to God, we are a threat to evil. That holy washing frees us from sin, death and the devil. At our baptism the Holy Spirit becomes our constant life companion, present always to gather us with other believers, enlighten us, strengthen our faith, as understood from the third article of the Apostles' Creed. The Holy Spirit is our gift, our comfort, and our advocate (John 14:6). But just as Jesus was baptized and led into the wilderness, we too are baptized and sent into the world, a world that is not always safe, just, or predictable. But likewise, at our baptism, the devil becomes our lifelong enemy. As Luther put it, "You have to realize that it is no joke at all to take action against the devil and not only to drive him away from the little child but also to hang around the child's neck such a mighty, life-long enemy."[3]

Paul put it in terms of spiritual warfare, a phrase that is used frequently within Evangelical circles today but less so among Lutherans. Paul recognized the evil forces that faced the church of his time, and indeed, continue to face the church today. He encouraged the first-century Christians in Ephesus to "put on the whole armor of God, so that you may be able to stand against the wiles of the devil. For our struggle is not against enemies of blood and flesh, but against the rulers, against the authorities, against the cosmic powers of this present darkness against the spiritual forces of evil in the heavenly places" (Eph. 6:11-12). Luther, too, recognized the existence of evil forces, the devil, and our need for protection and deliverance, writing about it in his morning and evening prayers:

I give thanks to you, my heavenly Father through Jesus Christ your dear Son, that you have protected me this night from all harm and danger, and I ask you that you would also protect me today from sin and all evil, so that my life and actions may please you completely. For into your hands I commend myself: my body, my soul, and all that is mine. Let your holy angel be with me, so that the wicked foe may have no power over me. Amen.[4]

While our prayers may not provide an immediate escape from evil or harm, we know nonetheless that God's love expressed in Jesus Christ is ours. In his letter to the Romans, Paul mused about what might separate us from Christ's love: hardship or distress, persecution, hunger, danger? He answered with an emphatic *no*, saying that we are more than conquerors (Rom. 8:35-37). Paul's next words are a passage that we offer as comfort to those who grieve, assurance to those in pain: "For I am convinced that neither death, nor life, nor angels, nor rulers, nor things present, nor things to come, nor powers, nor height, nor depth, nor anything else in all creation, will be able to separate us from the love of God in Christ Jesus our Lord" (Rom. 8:38-39). Nothing can separate us. Not fear, not evil, not doubt—nothing in all of creation.

Keep Us from Evil

There is yet one more way to look at this petition. We might consider that when we pray, "deliver us from evil," we ask God to keep us from doing what is evil. As we pray at the crossroads, it is important to take into account what impact our decisions will have. When trying to discern God's will and the direction God might have us take, we need to pay close attention to what perpetuates good, not evil. In other words, if our decision causes or perpetuates any evil in the world, then it likely is not God's will. It makes no sense to pray "deliver us from evil," if the path we take increases or ignores the poverty of another, or if our decision puts someone in harm's way or causes the tragedy that breaks another's heart. That is not to say all decisions will be clear-cut or that our actions will not cause another person angst. For instance, after years of caring for her parents at home, Martha finally made the gut-wrenching decision to place her mother in a nursing home. Her father, still alert and able to help himself with minor tasks, was lost and somewhat depressed with his wife out of the house. Martha herself experienced guilt pangs. Yet her mother was safe at the nursing home and was now cared for around the clock. Every decision requires give and take, requires a consideration of the positive and negative impact. Still we pray, "deliver us from evil," and in the process, keep us from being the evil from which another person needs deliverance.

Connecting with God's Word

Read Exodus 14. The Israelites had lived as slaves to the Pharaoh; they had experienced horrible plagues and eaten the first Passover meal on the run for their lives. And now Moses and the Israelites were at another dramatic crossroads. Ahead of them, ferocious surf, certain to lead to their deaths; behind them, Pharaoh and his army. "As Pharaoh drew near, the Israelites looked back, and there were the Egyptians advancing on them. In great fear, the Israelites cried out to the Lord" (Exod. 14:10). Sometimes as a decision looms before us, we feel as if we are looking for the lesser of two evils. Neither direction seems particularly appealing, and both have obvious drawbacks. What difference does it make to know you can call on the Lord at any time in any circumstance?

In the Exodus account, God literally made a way clear for the Israelites. God not only made the right decision obvious but also parted the sea so there was clear passage to the other side. How do you see God clearing a path for you and showing you the way?

Considering the Crossroads

1. What threatens your faith? What blocks your ability to be in deeper relationship with God?
2. Do you believe that God, the epitome of good, has defeated (and will ultimately defeat) the forces of evil? How does your answer impact the decision in front of you?
3. Think of the choices before you. Which choice potentially draws you closer to God? Which choice threatens to push God away?

For the kingdom, the power, and the glory are yours, now and forever. . . .

10

Praying into Infinity

As a rabid sports fan, I have become fascinated with how teams and players respond to phenomenal plays and wins. Professional football players seem particularly expressive to me. One player slams the ball into the ground, punches the air, and mugs for the camera. Another player nods his head emphatically and tosses the ball to an appreciative fan in the stands. Then there are those who provide moments of sheer entertainment. One player struts like a rooster, ending with a dramatic, low bow to opposing fans. Another player pumps the air, then beats on his chest, acknowledging his supreme greatness. Another does a high-step dance and bumps chests with a teammate. There seems to be no end to the creativity of expression as players take full credit for each positive and productive moment in the game. But what about the player who falls to a knee and points heavenward? What about the player who comes out of a huddle crossing himself? Are they giving God credit, or is it a form of show or superstition?

Countercultural Praying

While it may be entertaining in sports, self-glorification is in direct opposition to how we are taught to pray. We are cautioned about making a public show of our prayers at all. In Matthew, chapter 6, just before Jesus taught his disciples the Lord's Prayer, he reminded them that when they prayed they were not to draw attention to themselves, like those who by their words or actions think they will be heard. "Do not be like them," Jesus counseled (Matt. 6:8). Now, as we come to the end of the Lord's Prayer we find, as we did in the first petition, that the focus is not on ourselves at all. The focus is on God. Before we ever breathe an "amen," we verbally recognize that power belongs to God, not to us. Glory and praise are to be given to God, not to the one who is praying.

I believe this frees us in our decision-making. As forgiven people, we are free to make decisions and even free to fail, knowing that God loves us just the same. If the power and glory and credit for our successes truly belong to God, it could free us to be daring. Instead of fearing "what if I fail?" we might dare to think, "I'll try. Who knows? It might succeed." Several years ago a struggling city congregation invited another congregation to meet for conversation and prayer. The Synod had encouraged the two to yoke about ten years earlier, to no avail. Leaders were not even sure the two groups would meet. Within nine months of that initial meeting, the two congregations voted to unite as one. A year later they voted to merge and celebrated with the bishop and community's clergy. Throughout the merger they were led by a first-call pastor with no transitional ministry experience. The credit goes to God. What if it succeeds?

Jesus' final words before he gave his followers the Lord's Prayer in Matthew, were, "Your Father knows what you need before you ask him" (Matt. 6:8). While some might use this as an excuse never to pray, I think, on the contrary, it frees us to be more honest in our prayers and to be more confident in our decision-making. In the above-mentioned merger, I was the first-call pastor standing at a crossroads with the two congregations. Had it been up to me, the process would have been slow and deliberate. In retrospect, God had begun planting seeds for this merger ten years or more before it ever happened. So maybe as we prayed for guidance, our prayers were indeed familiar to God, who knew what we needed before we prayed it.

"For the kingdom, the power, and the glory are yours, now and forever." This last portion of the prayer, commonly known as "the doxology," means that we end where we began, with a recognition and declaration that God is God and God is in charge. While this portion of the prayer is not part of the original Greek text, I include it because it is part of what we commonly pray together and it focuses us on the center of the prayer: God. What's more, whatever the results of our prayer, any power or glory or praise is not ours to claim and strut, but is, in fact, due to God. This thinking is countercultural, for in our world, we associate power with money, with being the manager or supervisor of many; with politics and being in charge. In our world, glory is for the famous, for those who attract the attention of the paparazzi. Glory is reflected in someone's income, in the car they drive, and the jewelry they wear. Power and glory are goals that humans define, that humans measure, and that humans think they can attain. But the Lord's Prayer reverses this concept. The Lord's Prayer gives the power and glory to God, not just in a moment of thanks and celebration, but forever.

In Roman Catholic tradition, the worshiping community ends with "deliver us from evil," and at that point the priest adds petitions or expands on the theme of the particular mass. Only when the priest says, "for the kingdom, the power, and glory are yours" do the people respond with an "amen." To me, it seems that allowing these words to come from the lips of all people who are gathered, better reflects the spirit of the Lord's Prayer in general and allows us to end as we began, praying within community. It helps us focus on God's action, not ours. After all, it is the *Lord's* Prayer.

Amen! Amen!

As the Lord's Prayer ends, there is a trio of good, positive concepts: *power, glory* and *amen*. As we have discussed, the first two are easily abused within our human community. But the last word—*amen*—is a punctuation mark of the positive. "It's all good." That phrase can mean a myriad of things. It can be the answer to, "How are you?" It can be the closing comment after argument and reconciliation. It can be a way to greet the day. It can be a pep talk in hopes that saying it will make it true. When it comes to praying the Lord's Prayer, the words of the prayer are not based on hope; we do not cross our fingers, cling to a good-luck charm and make a wish. Instead, we end with a resounding cheer: "Yes!" As Luther said in the Small Catechism, "Amen, amen means 'Yes, yes, it is going to come about just like this.'"[1] One little word that many people just say by rote or habit and never even think of in terms of what it means; one little word reflects our belief that we are heard. In Luther's understanding, amen itself becomes a statement of faith. "This word is nothing else than an unquestioning word of faith on the part of the one who does not pray as a matter of luck, but knows that God does not lie because he has promised to grant it. Where there is no faith like this, there also can be no true prayer."[2]

In *A Simple Way to Pray*, written to his barber in 1535, Luther linked certainty, indeed absence of doubt, to the one word, amen: "Never doubt that God in his mercy will surely hear you and say 'yes' to your prayers. . . .Do not leave your prayer without having said or thought, 'Very well, God has heard my prayer; this I know as a certainty and a truth.' This is what Amen means."[3] It would seem, then, that our prayer could actually begin where it ends, with a moment of faith and affirmation that we will be heard. Just as we begin affirming our relationship to God by calling God Father, so too we affirm the same relationship by saying, amen. If you think about it, that one, solitary word, could stand as a prayer: "Amen. Yes! Let it be so." One word affirms our belief in God, our turning to God in prayer, our affirmation that God is in charge and is ready to help us when we call. We can express our questions and concerns, we can confess our need for direction and ask for God's guidance with the full understanding that God will hear us and respond. While working on a seminary project, presenting the Lord's Prayer to toddlers, I wrote, "I know you listen, God, because you promised. You hear my prayer and you will answer. I am happy!" That is the essence of amen: a word of joy and certainty sent God's way no matter what words precede it.

In the same way that confirmation allows the believer to affirm personally the promises made on his or her behalf at baptism, amen allows the believer who prays to affirm the one to whom we pray, the faith behind the prayer and the trust that there will be an answer. Just as confirmation is our yes to baptism, amen is our yes to God, our yes to all we have prayed, our yes to knowing we are heard. One of the things I love about many African-American worship styles is the call and response, the interaction between speaker and people. A friend explained that the amen spoken or shouted aloud is not random. It is the encouragement for the preacher to continue. It is the affirmation of what has just been said. It is a reminder that the preacher is not alone. It is not hard, after preaching in such a church to come away with more energy and renewed faith. It is not hard for me to imagine God, listening to me pray, waiting for my amen.

Amen at the Get-Go

What might it be like to begin our prayer with amen? To begin with a resounding yes to God and to prayer? To begin by affirming that God participates, interacts somehow, in this faith action? What might it be like to begin our discernment process with amen and then move directly to giving God the power and the glory, to acknowledging that God's kingdom is now and forever? It could change the entire way we approach decision making *and* prayer. Instead of coming with our hesitancy and our doubt, with a sense of being overwhelmed, we begin with a positive declaration. "Amen," after all, brings us back around to the exact same point we began when we prayed, "Our Father in heaven." We began with our attention on God, and end at the same place. In every decision yet to make, the crossroads lie between those two points, somewhere between turning to God and giving God the credit. The first few words of the Lord's Prayer and the amen at the very end are our bookends. We begin and end at the same place. We acknowledge that God is in charge and we are not God. We acknowledge that God is holy and we call to God in faith. We rest in the assurance that God listens and answers, and in faith we give God the credit. Amen! Whatever the answer to prayer, whatever the decision, "Amen! Let it be so."

Connecting with God's Word

Read Luke 17:11-19. In this passage, Jesus saw the lepers and responded to their need, to their cries for mercy. The lepers, as they left Jesus' presence, saw tangible signs of their healing. How do you see the world, your faith, and your current situation? Are you a glass half-empty person or a glass half-full person? How does your answer affect your day-to-day attitude and decisions?

All ten lepers cried out and all ten lepers were healed. What do you think motivated the one to return, praise God and give thanks? How do you think his life was different from the other nine from that moment on? What is the relationship between attitude and faith? If you were Jesus, what would your response to the ten be? What would be the follow-up to this story?

Considering the Crossroads

1. What motivates you to say thank you? How might thanking God for your blessings free you to make a faithful decision?
2. If the power, the glory, the credit and kudos for a good job or a solid decision belongs to God, how might you approach the choices differently?
3. Is there anything in your decision-making process right now that you can affirm and express joy? What is your amen on this day?

Conclusion: One Last Amen

I have been blessed to see anew how the Lord's Prayer ministers personally to people who are at various crossroads in their lives and their faith. To the parents of a newborn, it can be a thank-you and a reassurance of the energy and means they need to take care of an infant. To the children of a loved one in intensive care, it is whispered as a final plea, a final faith statement. At the graveside, it is a unifying blessing for the living. On Easter it is prayed boldly, as proclamation, while on Good Friday, we can barely hear each other pray. To a senior, it brings comfort, like a familiar face or a favorite blanket. To a young child, it is a moment of inclusion when they join the communion of saints in prayer. At the end of a council meeting, it is the resounding amen to all that has been accomplished.

There is something in these observations that convince me that this prayer is more than a specific set of words. It is a guide and model, yes, but it is also, it seems, a magnifying glass for our lives. A moment can take on different clarity through the praying of this prayer. It is also a treasure that unifies us with Christians across the globe. As I've listened to voices crack and seen tears during this prayer, I am also convinced that in a few short lines, we find holy permission to express every emotion and reaction to life, putting it at the Father's feet. The friend of a murder victim can't bring herself to say, "Your will be done." The father sending his son to boot camp is unable to speak the words, "Save us from the time of trial." The one just laid off stumbles over, "Give us today our daily bread." And yet, even as they falter, the community that surrounds them continues the prayer, and lifts their angst to God. At the same time, the homebound one who sorely misses gathering with the community connects with them through this prayer.

There is a sense in which this prayer can reflect back to us the challenging crossroads we face. At the same time, our crossroads can make the prayer more real. Might the young star athlete consider the prayer's doxology as she prepares for an interview? Might the words "thy will be done" be considered by family members as they gather in a hospital room and grapple with the decision to remove a ventilator from a loved one? The prayer gives voice to that for which we have no words. And time and again, the prayer's power to draw out honest emotion at the crossroads amazes me.

At the same time, we hope that the prayer might be a directional sign for us as we seek to discern God's will. Because there is so much at stake when we bring our worries and joys to God, I find it hard to pray the Lord's Prayer simply out of a sense of ritual or tradition. Even the placement of this prayer, I think, is not just ritual. In worship, as well as in other circumstances, it is offered at the conclusion of other prayers. By praying our intercessions and thanksgivings and then concluding with the Lord's Prayer, we are reminded of the way in which we are to pray and we are allowing the prayer itself to be an amen. The Lord's Prayer is the prayer that holds our petitions together in a unified verbal offering, much as seam binding holds the panels of a quilt together.

There is no magic in this prayer; no guarantee that an answer will be yes. But with Luther, "I am convinced that when a Christian rightly prays the Lord's Prayer at any time or uses any portion of it as he may desire, his praying is more than adequate. What is important for a good prayer is not many words, as Christ says in Matthew 6[:7], but rather a turning to God frequently and with heartfelt longing, and doing so without ceasing [1 Thess. 5:17]."[1] Amen! Let it be so.

Notes

Chapter 1

1. *Webster's II New College Dictionary* (Boston and New York: Houghton Mifflin, 2001).

2. Robert Kolb and Timothy Wengert, eds., *The Book of Concord: The Confessions of the Evangelical Lutheran Church* (Minneapolis: Augsburg Fortress, 2000), 444-445.

Chapter 2

1. *Merriam-Webster Online Dictionary*, www.merriam-webster.com/dictionary/mysticism (accessed February 2008).

2. Robert Kolb and Timothy Wengert, eds., *The Book of Concord: The Confessions of the Evangelical Lutheran Church* (Minneapolis: Augsburg Fortress, 2000), 354.2.

Chapter 3

1. Robert Kolb and Timothy Wengert, eds., *The Book of Concord: The Confessions of the Evangelical Lutheran Church* (Minneapolis: Augsburg Fortress, 2000), 445.37.

2. Ibid., 442.15.

3. Ibid., 445.41-43.

4. Wengert, Timothy J., trans. *A Contemporary Translation of Luther's Small Catechism: Study Edition* (Minneapolis: Augsburg Fortress, 1994), 29.

5. Kolb and Wengert, eds., *The Book of Concord*, 393.53.

6. Wengert, *Luther's Small Catechism*, 25.

7. Ibid., 32.

Chapter 4

1. Robert Kolb and Timothy Wengert, eds., *The Book of Concord: The Confessions of the Evangelical Lutheran Church* (Minneapolis: Augsburg Fortress, 2000), 447.53.

Chapter 5

1. Robert Kolb and Timothy Wengert, eds., *The Book of Concord: The Confessions of the Evangelical Lutheran Church* (Minneapolis: Augsburg Fortress, 2000), 448.61-62, 449.67.

Chapter 6

1. Robert Kolb and Timothy Wengert, eds., *The Book of Concord: The Confessions of the Evangelical Lutheran Church* (Minneapolis: Augsburg Fortress, 2000), 450.72.

2. Ibid., 450.74.

Chapter 7

1. Robert Kolb and Timothy Wengert, eds., *The Book of Concord: The Confessions of the Evangelical Lutheran Church* (Minneapolis: Augsburg Fortress, 2000), 452.92-453.92.

2. Ibid., 453.93.

3. Ibid., 452.89.

4. Ibid., 453.94.

5. Wengert, Timothy J., trans. *A Contemporary Translation of Luther's Small Catechism: Study Edition* (Minneapolis: Augsburg Fortress, 1994), 42.

Chapter 8

1. Curious George is a likeable, mischief-prone monkey featured in a 1973 book by the same name. Author: Hans Augusto Rey; published by Houghton Mifflin Co.

2. Robert Kolb and Timothy Wengert, eds., *The Book of Concord: The Confessions of the Evangelical Lutheran Church* (Minneapolis: Augsburg Fortress, 2000), 453.100.

3. Martin Luther, *Luther's Works Volume 42: Devotional Writings I* (Philadelphia; Fortress Press, 1969), 71.

4. Kolb and Wengert, eds., *The Book of Concord*, 454.102.

5. Ibid., 454.104.

6. Ibid., 454.106 and 455.111.

Chapter 9

1. Robert Kolb and Timothy Wengert, eds., *The Book of Concord: The Confessions of the Evangelical Lutheran Church* (Minneapolis: Augsburg Fortress, 2000), 455.113.

2. Ibid., 455.115.

3. Ibid., 372.3.

4. Ibid., 362.3.

Chapter 10

1. Wengert, *Luther's Small Catechism*, 40.

2. Robert Kolb and Timothy Wengert, eds., *The Book of Concord: The Confessions of the Evangelical Lutheran Church* (Minneapolis: Augsburg Fortress, 2000), 456.120.

3. Martin Luther, *Luther's Works, Volume 43: Devotional Writings II* (Philadelphia: Fortress Press, 1968), 198.

Conclusion

1. Martin Luther, *Luther's Works, Volume 43: Devotional Writings II* (Philadelphia: Fortress Press, 1968), Vol. 43, 12.

Additional Resources

Materials for a single or multiple session study of *On Earth as in Heaven* are downloadable free of charge at www.augsburgfortress.org/braun.

Bastien, Peter E. *Praying with Martin Luther* (Winona, Minn.: St. Mary's, 1999).
This prayer companion contains fifteen meditations based on stories about Martin Luther and his writings. Helpful for both personal use and with groups, it is part of the Companions for the Journey series from St. Mary's Press, which includes volumes on praying with a number of well-known Christians throughout history.

Bennethum, Michael. *Listen! God is Calling! Luther Speaks of Vocation, Faith and Work* (Minneapolis: Augsburg Fortress, 2003).
In this title from the Lutheran Voices Series, Pastor Bennethum speaks to pastors who are trying to help members apply their faith to their daily lives. An excellent resource for developing the skills necessary to listen for God's call in all aspects of life, the book is helpful for clergy and laypersons alike.

Johnson, Ben Campbell. *Discerning God's Will* (Louisville, Ky.: Westminster/John Knox, 1990).
Professor Emeritus of Christian Spirituality at Columbia Theological Seminary, Ben Campbell Johnson discusses how the search for personal meaning in life goes hand in hand with discerning God's will, something he proposes happens within the church as a "community of discernment." The book also contains a brief guide to the process of discernment, and each chapter includes helpful reflection exercises.

Listening for God, Volumes 1-4 (Minneapolis: Augsburg Fortress, 1994-2003).
A four-volume series designed for group use that helps participants realize the presence of God in many places and relationships. Each volume includes excerpts from the works of eight contemporary American authors, supplemented by author profiles, reflection questions, and a companion video.

Melander, Rochelle and Eppley, Harold. *Our Lives are Not our Own: Saying Yes to God* (Minneapolis: Augsburg Fortress, 2003).
    This book from the Lutheran Voices Series is designed to encourage personal reflection and create dialogue about God's call to a life of accountability and service. Contrary to popular culture's obsession with the individual, the message of this book is that God's unconditional love frees us from ourselves and gives us courage to live out our baptismal calling. Helpful for small-group and individual use.

Oswald, Roy M., Friedrich, Robert E. Jr. *Discerning Your Congregation's Future: A Strategic and Spiritual Approach* (Herndon, Va.: Alban Institute; 1996).
    A step-by-step guide to congregational planning that grounds strategic-planning techniques in a process of spiritual discernment. Encourages members to own the vision and be eager to participate in the congregation's calling, life, and ministry. Includes theory and practical applications.

Palmer, Parker J. *Let Your Life Speak: Listening for the Voice of Vocation* (Hoboken, N.J.: John Wiley & Sons, 2000).
    With understanding and gentle humor, Parker J. Palmer invites readers to listen with introspection and self-awareness to their inner voice and follow its leadings toward a sense of meaning and purpose. Using stories from his own life and the lives of others who have made a difference, the author shares insights gained from darkness and depression as well as fulfillment and joy.

Weatherhead, Leslie D. *The Will of God* (New York: Hyperion, 1990).
    This little book came from five sermons on understanding the will of God preached by Leslie Weatherhead during World War II for the congregation at City Temple in London. The book has helped hundreds of thousands of Christians explore how God's will is related to God's character and ultimate intentions for us.

Wengert, Timothy J., trans. *A Contemporary Translation of Luther's Small Catechism: Study Edition* (Minneapolis: Augsburg Fortress, 1994).
    This volume is a helpful, modern translation of Luther's explanations along with other catechetical study helps, such as prayers, worship rites, and Luther's introduction. New Revised Standard Version and Lutheran Book of Worship texts are used for the wording of the Ten Commandments, Lord's Prayer, Apostles' Creed, and the included worship rites.